# Caregiver's Gethsemane

## When a Loved One Longs To Die

### Cecile Bauer

PAULIST PRESS
New York/Mahwah, N.J.

The publisher gratefully acknowledges the use of excerpts from the *Order of Christian Funerals* © 1985, International Committee on English in the Liturgy, Inc. All rights reserved.

Cover Design by James F. Brisson.

Library of Congress Cataloging-in-Publication Data

Bauer, Cecile.
    Caregiver's gethsemane : when a loved one longs to die  /
    p.  cm.
    ISBN 0-8091-3572-8
    1. Caregivers—Prayer-books and devotions—English.  2. Terminal care—Religious aspects—Christianity.  3. Terminally ill—Family relationships.  4. Death—Religious aspects—Christianity.  5. Consolation. I. Title.
BV4910.9.B38  1995
259'.4—dc 20                                                          95-831
                                                                       CIP

Published by Paulist Press
997 Macarthur Boulevard
Mahwah, NJ 07430

Printed and bound in the
United States of America

# Contents

*Dedication*

To Beloved Victims, Now Victorious,
Mother and Joy

# Introduction

*"Father, if it is possible, let this cup pass me by."*
*Matthew 26:39*

No matter whether the patient is child, parent, sibling, or spouse, watching a loved one die is a personal Gethsemane. Even Christ, the God–Man, begged the Father for release as he prayed in the Garden of Olives. Caregivers also pray the patient will escape a painful death. It is especially agonizing when our loved one begs for the final release. "I've lived a good long life. It's time for me to die. Now! Do it!" The order is expected to be obeyed.

My loved one, always a strong feisty woman, was stricken with an incurable disease at age eighty-eight. This staunch woman told none of her family about her illness. Then a coma brought on by an overdose of pain medication put her in the hospital overnight. Summoned from across the continent by family members, my husband and I hastened to her side to be the daily caregivers.

We had no idea how severely our faith in God's mercy would be tested, or how difficult it would be to say no when our loved one begged to die. *Caregiver's Gethsemane*, a faith journey through the valley of death, was written to strengthen others.

# Chapter 1

*"Hear... the sound of my call; have pity on me, and answer me. Your presence, I seek....You are my helper; cast me not off; forsake me not, O God my savior."*

Psalm 27:7-9

In many of his psalm songs, King David sought the strength and protection of God. Often surrounded by camps of powerful enemies, what else could the former shepherd boy do other than pray for help? When the approaching death of a loved one calls us to be caregivers, it makes us feel kinship with David. We too feel overwhelmed by circumstances and crisis.

The call to serve often shatters an otherwise peaceful routine.

> *In our case, an older sister telephones for help. "It's Mother. She's dying. The doctor gives her four to six months. You said you would come if we needed you..."*

When we hear that a loved one is suffering and dying, the call to be a caregiver is answered from the heart. Most people immediately accept the responsibilities without counting future cost. Few people realize just how heavy the burden, or how rich the blessings, of caring for a dying loved one.

*I speak without hesitation. "We're coming."*

The decision to serve is the first and most important step. God does not demand very much from us, just total acceptance of his will. Once we agree to serve him as a caregiver to the dying, the life-changing decisions that follow seem to fall into place.

We lean on the strengthening hand of Jesus to guide us through major decisions about finances, job leave, previous commitments, and traveling mode.

> *In our situation, we live on the balmy west coast. Our dying loved one lives in the frozen east. A continent divides us. For several reasons, financial and personal, flying is not an option.*
> *My sister asks, "When can we expect you?"*
> *"Tuesday. It takes four days to drive."*
> *The Lord knew we needed a time of grace. We will use that stretch of traveling time to pray for strength, to grieve, and to prepare for the challenges ahead.*

Caregivers are not always gifted with an extended "shock absorber" time. Some struggle with the shocking news in the stark immediacy of an intensive care unit, or in the impersonal silence of a hospital chapel. Icy numbness threatens as the terrible news sinks in. No time to ponder. Our loved one—dying? If we stop to think, we will be undone, locked into helpless grief, completely useless for the daunting tasks ahead. God in his mercy grants a weapon to cope with the unthinkable. Frenetic action is a response to extreme stress. So much to do, so little time.

> *Because our loved one is helpless, and expected to die within a matter of months, our caregiving must be a live-in arrangement.*

Other caregivers may fulfill their duties by sharing home visits with concerned relatives or friends. Yet none of us can just walk away from everyday commitments. Family responsibilities beckon. The rent and other bills never stop. Employed caregivers may need an emergency leave of absence from their job. Church duties (eucharist minister, scripture study leader, etc.) may need reassigning to others. Caregivers always seem to be chosen from the busiest group of people. We are all involved in a multitude of regular activities. Yet we cannot deny the needs of the dying to fulfill other duties.

> *I pack warm clothes, sweaters, winter coats, and boots. The thermometer outside reads 101°, but in the east the autumn nights will be cold, the days dark, with rain changing to sleet. I drag out the tire chains. No telling when we will be coming home.*

The phone calls come last. No matter how important our various activities may be, they will survive without our presence.

> *A difficult call goes to my husband's boss. Few employers like to grant leave on such short notice. Dave must quit his part-time job, a sacrifice made in the name of family duty. We are fortunate his retirement benefits cover our basic bills.*

Other caregivers struggle with serious financial problems as the need for constant care of the dying person takes precedence over the harsh reality of unpaid bills. Yet we know that the Lord will always take care of his own.

Why are the most difficult calls to family members? Telling them of our loved one's fatal illness makes the sad news even harder to take. When they weep for our beloved, we are grieved anew.

> *Evening brings Dave home to chaos. Suitcases, picnic coolers, boots and tire chains litter our living room. He looks at my exhausted face and opens his arms. I fall into them. Hours of busywork have weakened the wall damming my grief and fear. The curtain of denial protecting my turbulent emotions rips asunder. I weep.*

☙

*Lord, hear our desperate call for help. Surround us with your strength. Comfort us in our fear and sorrow. Show mercy for our loved one as he/she struggles with the final illness. Let your kindness and mercy flow through him/her. Be our helper when the day is long and we are weary. Forsake us not, O God our savior.*

# Chapter 2

*"Thereupon Mary set out, proceeding in haste to the hill country."*

Luke 1:39-40

Though the maiden Mary was newly pregnant by the grace of the Holy Spirit, she hastened to make the arduous journey to help her kinswoman Elizabeth. It could not have been easy for a young unmarried girl to travel the dangerous hills of Judah. Yet Mary did not hesitate to make the journey to help elderly Elizabeth, pregnant with the miracle child, John. Mary knew that we serve God by serving others in need. Her life is a perfect example of unselfish service.

> *At 6:00 a.m. Dave and I, accompanied by our old dog Ginger, hit the road east. I pray that we will follow Mary's example and serve our loved one well through the last days. My thoughts wander over the years of our relationship. We do not often agree, about anything. Mother is strong and stubborn. I am the meek obedient child. She rages and storms about. I dodge out of the way, smiling to cover my cringing heart. We have never been close. She loves me, though that love has never been openly expressed.*

Unresolved emotional conflicts between a caregiver and a dying person may cause problems. No matter how mature our faith, we always feel a certain amount of guilt as the death of our loved one draws near. *Did I cause this anguish, Lord? Is my loved one suffering because I failed to offer sufficient love?* Many of us remained locked into the magical thinking of our childhood when we believed an enemy would die if we wished for it. Others, raised by repressive parents, are afraid of being rebuffed by the older, colder generation, and never learn to freely express love. We must try to overcome the walls between us. Time is so short. Eternity beckons.

> *I pray for the strength and patience to be a caregiver. What if she refuses to take medication? What if she pitches a fit and throws us out of the house, again? Yet this time is different. This time, she needs us.*

The Sierra Mountains reflect crimson and silver in the rising sun.

> *I gaze at the unforgiving rocks and pray that my mother will not harden her heart this time. That she will accept our well-meant sacrifices and maybe even say, "I love you," before she is gone forever.*

The mountains level off and become the desert lands of Nevada.

> *I stare at the endless sagebrush and scrub growth. My heart feels as barren as this wilderness.*

Caregivers to the dying often struggle through a pre-grieving process. The emptiness and depression as the reality of our approaching loss finally hit us is a real desert experience. Now we may appreciate the forty days Jesus spent in the desert, fasting and praying. We wonder how he could stand the desolation.

❦

O Jesus, fill our hearts with understanding and acceptance. We long to do your will, to follow your paths, to truly love and honor our dying loved one. You know us inside and out, Lord. You know we are frightened of the heavy responsibility of caring for our loved one. We are also filled with guilt for old quarrels, still unresolved. We are not saintly people, Lord. Neither is our dying one. It will not be easy taking care of him/her. Please help.

Mary, Mother of us all, teach us your strength of character. We need to unselfishly give of ourselves as you did for Elizabeth. Pray that we will serve him/her as humble loving servants, not as disgruntled children. In Jesus' name, Amen.

# Chapter 3

*"What did you go out to the wasteland to see—a reed swaying in the wind? Tell me, what did you go out to see...?"*

*Matthew 11:7-8*

Jesus spoke to the crowds about John the Baptist, a holy prophet who lived in the desert eating only wild honey and locusts. John dedicated his life to preparing a path for "one more powerful than I...to come after me. I am not fit to stoop and untie his sandal straps." John's preaching brought crowds of people to the barren desert. Some of them suffered disappointment because of his humble clothing and strong messages. They sought a dazzling Messiah. They found a rough-clothed hermit.

In biblical days, and even today, the desert is a place of quiet isolation where God may whisper to the listening heart. It is difficult to travel through any desert without noticing the barren desolation. Nothing to comfort a seeking soul but beige rocks, bent and twisted shrubs, a reed shaken by the wind. No shouting prophet to make straight the paths of the Lord. Maybe God uses this absence of distractions to claim our full attention? *Is that you, Lord, trembling the sagebrush?*

*After driving through the barrens of Nevada and Utah, we stay overnight in a mountain rest stop in Wyoming. It is cozy sleeping in the back of the truck, the three of us snuggling up on an old camping mattress. We are grateful for the dog's warmth. Her animal heat defrosts our frozen toes. I awaken at 3:30 a.m., alert and ready to travel. Dave remains sleeping in the back. I drive through the high desert of Wyoming. The interstate is empty of traffic except for occasional trucks. They fly past, their tires singing, running lights flickering a friendly hello.*

The rising sun stains rocks and desert shrubs a luminous silver. Just before the flaming ball peeks over the horizon, the silver light changes to a luminous pink. The empty desert world reflects the miracle of a new day. This unexpected beauty lifts our hearts with joy. Surely the Creator who transforms this desolation with such shining beauty will also use his tremendous power to heal our loved one?

*I find myself deep in silent conversation, arguing with God. Surely, Father, it must be some mistake? Our loved one does not deserve such a cruel punishment! How can she be stricken with that dread disease? We always knew she would die someday, Lord. But not this way! Please not this terrible agony. Our loved one doesn't deserve this and you know it!*

Anger at God is a common reaction to the shock and grief of an approaching death. So also is bargaining with the Creator of life. Surely the God of mercy will save our loved one the terrible torment of dying from a crippling illness? If storming heaven will obtain a pardon from the death sentence, our loved one may be healed by sheer persistent prayer.

*The sun clears the eastern horizon. The glowing silver and crimson light fades. The barren land is again a moonscape* of desolation. Sagebrush trembles in the wind. My heart quivers with anticipation of grief.

❧

Father, when we dare to make demands on your mercy, remind us of the lonely reed swaying in the wind. We have no more power over life and death than these puny plants. Fill our frightened souls with acceptance of your will. For only by surrendering to your plan for our loved one's life may we find peace and fullness of heart. "Tell me, what did you go out to see?" Let us see, and accept, your will, O Lord.

# Chapter 4

*"Not a single sparrow falls to the ground without your Father's consent."*

*Matthew 10:29*

Jesus instructed his apostles to be courageous as they left on their first missionary journey. They were to take only the bare necessities and trust in God to provide for their needs.

Caregivers may notice many parallels in their faith journey as they approach the great unknown of a loved one's last illness. We travel light and trust in God's generosity to provide what we need.

> *In our case, we have barely enough gas money for the trip. Our food supply is running low. Our clothing is much too thin for the icy blasts of the east. Still, we press on. Our loved one needs us.*

Strong is the bond of love that draws ordinary people into extraordinary service. Caregivers give up personal comfort, financial security, and a big chunk of time to serve a dying loved one. When worldly concerns threaten to overwhelm our good intentions, we find reassurance in scripture. "Do not be concerned. You are worth far more than a flock of sparrows."

> *By alternating drivers we reach Nebraska by evening. We bed down in a busy rest stop. Travelers whiz past and shake*

*our cozy nest in the back of our truck. I sleep fitfully and awaken to the sleepy chatter of birds. Ginger is dancing, eager for her morning run. My heart gives a sad little ping as she wriggles in my arms. Just last year she was frisky enough to make the leap from truck bed to ground. Now she needs lifting down, another reminder of encroaching old age. I wonder: How many more trips for poor old Ginger? A stab in my heart reminds me that our loved one will never travel again either.*

The approach of a loved one's death is a series of losses. Some are huge (how will we survive without our loved one?). Some are tiny and overlooked, at first. The familiar voice on the telephone chatting about family celebrations. The unexpected visit. A strong hug of greeting. The sympathetic ear sharing our triumphs or sorrows. Someone to marvel over extra snapshots. Dying people turn ever inward as the final victory approaches. We lose pieces of our loved ones in countless ways before they are truly gone forever.

*Ginger sets a brisk pace as we trot to the dog-walk section of the rest stop. Suddenly, she is a pup again in the brisk early morning air, leaping, barking, grinning as we run together. Her enthusiasm surprises me. I trip over the leash and go down, skinning both hands, my chin, and an eyebrow. One finger feels numb. Great! Just what I needed. Quick tears of self-pity shame me. I am not really hurt, just humiliated. Ginger washes my scrapes with long healing licks. Her tawny eyes beg for forgiveness.*

❧

*O Father, when we stumble and fall like baby birds, pick us up and comfort us, for you are God of all creation,* full of mercy and kindness. Your Son assures us that we are worth more than an entire flock of sparrows. Teach us to rely on your mercy and strength, O Father. For your love is enough for us.

# Chapter 5

*"And may the gracious care of the Lord our God be ours; prosper the work of our hands for us!"*

*Psalm 90:17*

Psalm 90 is the beginning of the fourth book, a collection of songs and prayers describing God's eternity and human frailty. It could serve as a dedication prayer for new caregivers.

> *We arrive at our loved one's house. The invalid's physical appearance is shocking. No longer plump and sturdy, even her skin has lost its healthy glow. A waif in a faded robe sits in a favorite rocking chair. The seat is padded with a waterproof cover because the dying one wears diapers now. A wrinkled cheek lifts for a kiss. The dreadful suffering stare strikes like a physical blow. A question burns in the haunted depths of her eyes: Why me?*

Caregivers struggle with the same question. Why are some people stricken with dreadful diseases while others are spared? People of God know that suffering is not really a punishment. Yet when a particularly cruel disease like cancer or AIDS strikes down a loved one, it is so easy to slip into the familiar trap of: "Why, God? Why me?"

> *My middle sister hugs me with fierce relief. Her husband complains about the work of caring for our invalid. "I'm*

*here now, Mother. I'll take care of everything." Relief sparkles in her eyes. She sighs deeply as if shrugging off a burden too heavy for her frail shoulders. "Would you rather be in bed now?"*

*She nods. Numbly, trying not to think, I make ready her bed.*

Home health-care of a diapered invalid has many short-cuts. A lawn and leaf bag spread across the bottom sheet covers the hip area. A flat sheet, folded in half, is spread over the plastic for a draw sheet. "Chucks" (blue water-proof squares used by hospitals to absorb urine and other wastes) also save on laundry. Now, if diapers leak, only the draw sheet needs changing.

*"Your bed is ready." Her shuffling gait pierces our hearts. It takes two of us to support the hunched body. The short walk to the bedroom seems endless. She sinks onto the edge of the bed and collapses backward. Is this the same person who, every morning for twenty years, walked a mile to church? Now a few shuffling steps leave her exhausted.*

It is a shock when a beloved one is reduced to helpless-ness by terminal illness. The strong person we turn to when-ever we need help has vanished. Instead, a bed-wetting, needy bundle of pain looks to us for help. Our hearts thump with fear. Can we fulfill the needs of our dying loved one? Just changing a diaper presents a challenge to modesty.

*My loved one was raised by strict Irish Catholic parents. Chastity meant no serious skin or body parts revealed. I had never seen her unclothed. She taught us to follow her chaste example. Now we must somehow overcome mutual embar-rassment and change her.*

Adult children who care for dying parents agree that personal hygiene is a tough problem to overcome. The patient may weep after losing control of the bladder. The caregiver weeps because this loss of control also means a loss of our loved one's personal dignity. Cleaning up is the easy part. Even a queasy person can get the job done by approaching the waste matter as just another food by-product. In one end, out the other. Overcoming false modesty is the tough challenge.

> *Our loved one solves this problem by reverting to early childhood. When we lift the edge of the nightgown, her legs spread like a newborn's. Appalled, we change the diaper quickly, trying to conceal shock.*

It is an emotional challenge when child/parent roles switch because of the neediness of fatal illness. Once this stumbling block is successfully overcome, it clears the path for a more comfortable caregiver/patient relationship.

> *After the diaper change, Mother gasps for breath. We prop her head and shoulders on pillows to ease her struggle. She closes her eyes. We tiptoe out.*

Caring for the dying is not only a matter of good nursing care. It becomes an altered lifestyle, a temporary vocation. From the moment of dedication (or acceptance), to the final release, the caregivers hold primary responsibility for the comfort of the dying loved one. For some people, the heavy duties require more than they can give.

> *I speak to my oldest sister on the telephone as middle sister Betty and her husband beat a hasty retreat. "If you need anything, let us know." The door slams behind them. Neither person has the experience, nor the stamina, to care*

*for an invalid. Too bad. They miss the last bittersweet days of caring for our precious one.*

Caregiving is both privilege and duty. Easing the physical pain and soothing the mental anguish come first. But listening and learning about life and love from someone who will soon be unavailable to enlighten us is a rare privilege.

❦

*Sweet Jesus, prosper the work of our hands as we face the challenges ahead. Teach us to be to be grateful for the strength of your love, and not to judge the weaknesses of other family members. Remind us that their love for our dying loved one is just as strong as ours.*

# Chapter 6

*"For sighing comes more readily to me than food, and my groans well forth like water. For what I fear overtakes me, and what I shrink from comes upon me."*

Job 3:24-25

Job is an upright man, blessed by God, whose faith is tested severely. His family and possessions are snatched away. Hideous sores cover his body. A grievously suffering person, he calls out to God for relief. Caregivers hear the echo of Job's groaning from the sickbed.

> *We are unpacking when Mother's moans of pain become shouts. We rush into the bedroom. She writhes on the pillows. Her eyes roll back in her head. Fists pound the blanket. "Make it go away! Make it stop!"*
> *"Do you have pain pills, Mother?" She shakes her head.*
> *"How about a couple of aspirin?"*
> *"Anything! Make it go away!"*

Nothing prepares the caregiver for the feeling of complete helplessness as our loved one writhes in pain. We want to do something, anything, to ease the suffering. Too often, the weapons to relieve serious pain are shockingly unavailable.

*Her fists strike her upper chest again and again. I run to fetch aspirin and a glass of water. Dave supports her shoulders. I drop the pills into her mouth and offer a sip of water. She chews the pills! My throat burns thinking about the hot grainy taste of chewed aspirin. After a tiny sip of water, she sinks back against the pillows. When her breathing grows quiet, we leave her alone to sleep. Minutes later, she shouts again for help.*

Panic is a constant enemy in the battle against pain. Caregivers feel terribly helpless when their loved one shouts for relief.

*"Would you be more comfortable sitting in your chair?" She nods. We help her into the living room. Moments later, she begins to convulse.*

A full body seizure by a homebound invalid is a signal for professional help.

*Dave calls 911. An ambulance arrives. People in tan uniforms crowd the tiny living room. Machines pop out of satchels and metal boxes. Wires snake from the machines to monitor heartbeat and pulse. The woman in charge of the paramedics takes me aside. When I mention Mother's fatal illness and describe her seizure, they take her off to the hospital.*

It is not a weakness of commitment to temporarily relinquish the care of a dying loved one to professionals. Ordinary people, called to be caregivers, know the limitations of their skills.

*In our case, our loved one needed serious pain management, available only in a hospital setting. My oldest sister Joy and her husband Ed meet us at the hospital. She is pale and thin after completing a course of chemotherapy. Her face, carved with new lines of worry, smiles with relief when she sees us. She hugs both of us. "Thank God you're here! I didn't know what to do. I can't take care of mother, and Betty..."*

"We're here now. We'll stay as long as necessary."

What would families do if no one stepped forward to be the caregiver? It is such a tough vocation. Many believe that caring for the dying has no success stories, that in the end someone always dies. Why volunteer for the agony of watching? Christians believe that to comfort the sick and dying is a blessed way of the cross. Like our suffering Christ, we feel chosen to serve.

*The hospital admits Mother for tests and treatment. She sleeps comfortably from pain medication they give her. We kiss her goodbye, a tiny, gray stranger now in the care of professionals. We return to my childhood home, and settle in for the long haul.*

☙

*Jesus, fountain of strength, please help us in the days ahead. It will not be easy to be caregivers. Our loved one is so needy. His/her groans of pain, like Job's, well forth like water. The cries of agony tear us apart. We are afraid witnessing the suffering will be too much to bear. Our souls shrink from the disease that has come upon him/her. Teach us how best to help him/her. Spirit of God, fill us with good thoughts and good works. We can do nothing without your help, O Lord Jesus Christ.*

# Chapter 7

*"Wait for the Lord with courage; be stout-hearted,
and wait for the Lord."*

*Psalm 27:14*

Surrounded by enemies, King David prays for courage. It could not have been easy for the beleaguered leader, yet he remained steadfast. Caregivers may feel kinship with frightened David. We too become surrounded by the enemy of our loved one's fatal illness. We pray desperately for help, overwhelmed by the sick person's helpless dependence on us. Caregivers feel impatient for God to act now, on our terms. *Are you paying attention, God? We need help, NOW!*

> *Our hearts are heavy as we go to the hospital to visit Mother. She is quiet and peaceful now with an I.V. draining glucose and pain medication into her system. She accepts very little food. Her glittering gaze wanders over my face. She beckons me closer. Her moist whisper tickles my ear. "I signed a 'Do Not Resuscitate' order today," she says.*

Why is it such a blow to realize our loved one accepts the approaching death and is ready to leave us? We are not ready to let go.

> *I blink away tears. She snorts. Her lips tighten. "I've lived a good long life. Do you really think I want to go on hooked up like this?" She shakes her arm with the I.V. apparatus. A*

*buzzer goes off. A nurse rushes in and resets a button on the machine hooked up to Mother's I.V. line. She glances from the patient to me and touches my arm. "Could I see you outside?" We step into the hallway. Dave takes my hand. The nurse stares at our faces. "You do know Mrs. Ramier is terminal." It is not a question. We both nod. The nurse takes a deep breath. "You will be her caregivers at home?"*

The decision to accept the care of a dying loved one is taken seriously in the world of professional health care. Hospitals may refuse to release a dying patient until arrangements for outside care are complete.

*We nod our willingness to be caregivers. "Have you thought about joining the Hospice Program?" Dave glances at me. "We haven't discussed it yet. My sister Joy usually makes the major family decisions," I say. Dave says, "What is the Hospice Program?" The nurse makes a note on her chart. "I'm going to contact a Hospice worker so she can explain the program. Let me know what you decide before we release the patient."*

The Hospice Program is an organization of health-care professionals dedicated to allowing terminal patients to die at home. Caregivers, new to the program, have many misgivings about the heavy responsibilities. What will happen when we take the patient home? Can we make our loved one comfortable enough? The possibility of pain deepening into unabated agony terrifies us. What will we do if a parent, always a pillar of strength, shrieks aloud and begs for relief? We feel frightened, trapped.

*In our case, the memory of Mother's astonishing cries last night (was it only last night?) fills us with dread for the future.*

Feelings of inadequacy are common among caregivers. The need for complete care, the bathing, feeding, and medicating, builds a tight emotional cage around us. No wonder we long to escape.

> *Evening brings family to the hospital. We confer in the hallway. Joy announces that the doctors are doing exploratory surgery on Mother's lungs tomorrow. Everyone is upset. Why torture a dying old woman with elective surgery? Joy sighs. "There is always the chance..." Her voice trails away. Maybe she is thinking about her own desperate fight, four months of radiation treatments and six months of chemotherapy. Skin over bones, the outline of her backbone sticks through her cotton blouse. But the spine is stiff, ready to do battle with Mother's disease too. "We can't just give in!"*

Family members frequently become the last stumbling blocks to a loved one's peaceful death. We refuse to let go, holding on to shreds of hope long after the loved one is ready to die.

> *I say, "Mother is ready to die. She told me so this morning." Betty's face crumples. Joy looks away, biting her lip. The brothers-in-law stare at the floor, hands jammed into pockets, heads turned away from the pain written on our faces. Joy tries for a joke. "Guess what Mother told me this afternoon?" Her lips quiver. We wait for a cheerful punchline. Joy, our family comedian, doesn't let us down. "Mother told me not to waste money on a fancy casket. 'You know how frugal I've always been. Pick out something cheap!'"*

The surprising humor of family stories shared around a deathbed often shocks us. How can anyone laugh at a time like this? As our loved one slips into his arms, God gives us these family memories to draw us closer together.

❦

*Lord, when will we learn to accept your will? Surrounded by the enemies of painful disease and certain death, we call out to you like frightened children. Teach us the most difficult virtues: the patience to wait and the courage to accept your will with total trust. In Jesus' name, Amen.*

# Chapter 8

*"'I see an enemy's hand in this.' And the enemy... is the devil."*

*Matthew 13:28, 39*

Jesus tells the parable of the wheat farmer who sowed good seeds in his field. Trying to ruin the farmer (God), an enemy (the devil) sowed weeds in the same field. When the wheat sprang up, so did weeds. Rather than pull up the weeds and uproot the wheat plants also, God allows both good and bad to grow together. Jesus uses this story to explain the presence of evil in the world.

Caregivers may become tempted to blame God for evil weeds growing in our loved one's body. *How could you let this happen, God, to someone who has always been your faithful servant.* A loved one's painful illness often shakes our trust in a caring, protecting Father. It is so difficult to accept that God would allow the enemy to sow evil seeds. At night we toss and turn, hearts thumping, major muscles jerking, gearing up to fight the evil enemy. Ears prickle like a jungle cat's, alert for battle.

> *We find our fallen one wrapped in a gauze bonnet with tape around her wedding ring. Fear glitters in her sunken eyes. Her arms flail as an attendant slides her limp body across the bed onto a gurney. I tuck in a toe not covered by the*

*sheet. She pulls her foot away. "Don't forget, buy cheap!"*
*They whisk her away.*

Caregivers find that the longest hours are those spent outside an operating room locked into the terrifying uncertainty of prognosis. Sometimes we are too numb to even pray. Thank God the Spirit prays for us during those long silent agonies.

*The surgeon peels away his mask as he approaches us. We stand up. Bad news seems easier to take wrapped in each other's arms. The doctor shakes his head sadly. His words are not reassuring. "The patient's tumors are growing like a wildfire. Too late for aggressive treatment; the disease has spread to the brain." We fall silent at this latest blow. She has always been so bright and alert, proud of her memory and mental adroitness.*

When an enemy invades the center of our loved one's personhood, it seems an especially cruel blow. We cringe at the thought of the final days ahead and how our loved one will hate the realization of the decline of once vibrant mental powers.

*Dave and I sit a while longer, too numb to move on. He stares at his folded hands. My stunned thoughts lock on the dreadful disease. A brain tumor! I shudder with revulsion. Who did this terrible thing?* "An enemy has done this."

Caregivers, struggling with a terrible prognosis, feel tempted to scream at God for not protecting their loved one from this final degradation. How could a loving Father allow this rotting away of all that makes this person so safely familiar—the quirks, the silly frugality, the fierce indepen-

dence, the very special human mind? It is too much to bear.
Too much!

> *That afternoon, the Hospice worker sets up our meeting at*
> *the end of a quiet hallway. Joy and Ed, Dave and I listen to*
> *the future shape of our days. Ms. Smith, a woman with kind*
> *eyes, explains the program.*

Hospice is dedicated to the quality care of the dying provided by family members in a home setting. All sickroom
needs such as hospital beds, oxygen equipment, medication, and home visits by accredited physicians and nurses
are provided. The family provides the caregivers. Hospice
also gives important moral and spiritual support. Social
therapists interview the caregivers and suggest ways to
maintain their mental health. Priests, ministers, and rabbis
are on call for spiritual support. It is never easy to care for
the dying. Hospice is there every step of the way.

> *"Who will be the primary caregiver?" Ms. Smith asks. I*
> *shiver, contemplating the difficult days ahead. Someone*
> *must care for Mother. "We will," I say, with a nod toward*
> *Dave. "You understand that the patient is never left alone?"*
> *We both nod. When we sign the hospice form, Mother be-*
> *comes enrolled in the program. "Her regular doctor must*
> *sign a release form before we can proceed." We must look*
> *worried because Ms. Smith smiles. "Don't worry. Most doc-*
> *tors are happy to relinquish a dying patient to us. It's just a*
> *matter of catching the doctor for his signature." She hugs all*
> *of us. "We'll talk again. You made a good decision."*

Even after making all the right decisions concerning the
care of our loved one, we may not feel good about it. We
may still feel rebellious, puzzled, and angry with God for

allowing the "bad seeds" of terminal illness to invade our loved one.

❦

*Lord Jesus, help us to accept your teachings about good and evil. It is so hard to trust in a loving Father when our loved one is suffering from the enemy within. Weed out rebellious thoughts, O Lord. Plant only the good seeds of acceptance, trust and obedience in our hearts.*

# Chapter 9

*"Look toward me, and have pity on me, for I am alone and afflicted. Relieve the troubles of my heart and bring me out of my distress. Put an end to my affliction and my suffering...."*
Psalm 25:16-17

King David prays for protection and consolation. A robust man who falls into serious sin, David repents and returns to his God. Heavy of heart, he begs God to put an end to his suffering. Even as powerful a man as King David struggled with grief and loss. His best friend Jonathan (son of Saul), his beloved son Absalom, and the infant child born of his sin with Bathsheba all died before their time. *Even the king weeps.*

Caregivers may also feel helpless in the face of their loved one's approaching agony. We pray that God will strengthen us for the ordeal ahead. *Relieve our troubled hearts, O Lord.*

*After a fitful night's sleep, we awaken in my childhood bedroom. Flowered wallpaper decorates the slanted walls. In happier times, I was part of my parents' paperhanging team. We worked weekends papering rooms for friends. "Five dollars a room," Pop said, "and a buck for the kid." My father died twenty-two years ago. We still miss him. I cannot ac-*

*cept the thought:* soon Mother will join him. *Too painful right now.*

At the beginning of our caregiving mission, we cannot bear to think of the approaching death. Totally unacceptable! God will grant a cure. He must! We cling to our loved one and pray desperately, sometimes defiantly, for a miracle cure.

*I roll out of bed and begin a frantically busy day. The house needs a good cleaning.*

The vocation of caregiver is not just about good nursing skills. It is a comfort to the dying one if the surroundings are cheerful, free of clutter, and, hopefully, clean. Dark gloomy sickrooms give everyone a case of the weeps.

*Our hearts are heavy as we sort Mother's belongings. I feel like a sneak thief invading her fiercely guarded privacy as I pick through her possessions. It wrenches my heart to put the good dresses, skirts and blouses into storage bags. Ragged, urine-soaked clothing is tossed out. I feel as if I am throwing her away, forever, and she is not even dead yet!*

Sometimes it is difficult to realize that our dying loved one suffers not only from the pain of illness, but from the shame of helplessness. Caregivers, strong and willing to help, may not be sensitive enough to the crippled pride of our loved ones. We plunge in, good intentions worn like a shield, and take charge of the patients' life and possessions. No wonder they get cranky!

*In our case, a favorite ragged sweater, salvaged from Pop's closet and worn in his memory, cannot be saved. Joy and Ed buy an inexpensive living room suite to replace urine-*

*stained furniture. We could leave that room empty, but relatives will be visiting.*

When an older person dies, it is often the end of an era. Relatives and friends come to visit with mixed emotions. They feel sad at the approaching loss. Yet they remember fondly the parties of days gone by. Sometimes it makes people uncomfortable to remember the good times. Who will give the parties now? Will there be other celebrations, or are all the good times over?

*Dave assigns basement junk to three piles: good tools, questionable keepsakes, and trash. Mother's will directs that her house will be sold after her death. We are doing advance work now, so that after (I refuse to think, after the funeral), we may go right home.*

Caregivers may find that physical busywork comforts us. It not only keeps the body busy, it also keeps our minds from racing in the tight little trap of why, why, why?

*A system of family hospital visits evolves. Dave and I do lunch. Joy takes the late afternoon supper shift. Betty, who works during the day, visits during the evening, then comes over to mother's house to talk and unwind. Joy and Ed visit every evening also. Betty and Len, aware that my allergy to cigarette smoke will not allow them to smoke in the house, take frequent smoke breaks outside in the driveway.*

Caregivers have a primary duty to keep our own bodies in good health. We will need all our strength for the long haul ahead. It is not prudent to martyr ourselves for the needs of others.

*Our dog Ginger appreciates the company outside. She must be puzzled by the new house rules. She sleeps in the base-*

*ment now instead of beneath the kitchen table. Mother hates dogs. This is still Mother's house, and her wishes rule. Our faithful pet is banished to the basement with frequent forays outside with the smokers.*

❦

*Lord, comfort us in our distress. This is so hard, sorting through our loved one's things. We know they are only material things, not important to him/her now. We can take nothing when you call us home to heaven. Yet our heart aches for his/her many losses. Now the loss of independence seems the worst loss of all. Help us be a comfort, Lord. Let us be generous and giving, not grudging and impatient. Let your will be done, O Lord, not ours.*

# Chapter 10

*"Come to me, all you who are weary and find life burdensome, and I will refresh you."*
*Matthew 11:28*

Jesus comforts his followers, many of whom were overburdened by the strict religious rules of those days. He preached a simple creed of forgiveness, love for neighbor, and caring for others. He ignored hundreds of rules of ritual conduct.

The twin burdens of grief and fear may be overwhelming for caregivers. We can only pray for Jesus' love to strengthen us. He refreshes us with the blessings of family.

> *Between our hospital visits and house clearing work, we plan a family dinner. We are blessed with several adult children and grandchildren who live in the area. Six will come for a spaghetti dinner. I mix bread dough in the morning, and, while it is rising, walk to a local grocery store. Dave offers to drive but I prefer to snatch some outdoor exercise.*

Caregivers, new to the vocation, may not realize just how important fresh air and exercise may be to their physical and mental health. In the darkest hours of grief, even a brief breath of outside air refreshes the body and soul.

> *The family arrives for dinner. Adult children and grandchildren gladden our hearts as they inhale the food. A loaf of*

*fresh baked bread vanishes in an eyeblink. Dave jumps up to slice another loaf. He smiles at his sons' robust appetites, teases the grandchildren, and basks in the golden glow of a magic family meal. The crowded kitchen hums with conversation and laughter. Family jokes are told again for the benefit of grandchildren. They howl, adults grin.*

Family stories, shared with loved ones, are golden threads that bind us forever. It is important to maintain these family ties as the death of a loved one draws near. How will we cope if not supported by the arms of our remaining loved ones?

*After evening visiting hours, my brother's children, both college students, stop by the house. They look stunned. I take my nephew into the den to give him the flag from his father's funeral, a prized possession. It is kept partially unfurled, with my brother's medals displayed next to a picture of him in uniform. "Would you like your dad's flag?" I ask. He nods and reaches for the flag. I hear him gulp down a big lump in his throat. We fold it together. "Thanks," he whispers.*

Caregivers sometimes find it a difficult chore to disperse mementos. It feels as if we are giving away pieces of our loved one. Sometimes it is a pleasure, other times a painful event.

*In our case, it feels good to give away our loved one's precious keepsakes. We know they will be valued. We are gathering some things together for my niece too, but it will take a few more days. She nods and smiles nervously. "No hurry." She does not want to think about any inheritance from Grandma. Not now. Not yet.*

Many times it is the young who find mementos from a precious one too painful to accept. Older people seem to ac-

cept the keepsakes in the spirit they were intended, as re-
minders of a loved one, now gone on to God.

> *We return to the crowded living room and the spirited con-*
> *versation of family members. Everyone enjoys this relaxed*
> *evening. For a brief time, the deathwatch is suspended. For*
> *this one evening, we forget the hard days ahead, the difficult*
> *decisions, the impending loss. The company lingers until af-*
> *ter midnight. We sleep well this night.*

❧

*Lord, thank you for family. Their support helps to lift*
*us when sorrow would drag us down. Remind us to re-*
*member these happy times during the weary days ahead.*
*Thanks, Lord. We needed your healing touch to refresh us.*

# Chapter 11

*"Who is my mother?"*

*Matthew 12:48*

Jesus' relatives, aware that a crowd of non-believers wants to harm him, try to whisk him off to safety. When he learns his mother is seeking him, he refuses to accept her help. Faith in Jesus' prophetic words creates a relationship superior to that of mere human bonds, the Bible insists. Still, it is a difficult lesson. Does it mean caregivers are to turn their backs on dying relatives and serve Jesus another way?

> *In our case, did we do the wrong thing coming here? Will we serve Jesus better if we return home to our scripture study group and the eucharistic ministry?*

> *Are we missing something here, Jesus? Surely you did not mean that we are to abandon our loved ones when they are so needy?*

> *In our case, we feel strongly that this is our assigned role now, caregivers at my mother's side, working and praying until Jesus comes to take her home.*

It is a tempting idea, given the normal human reluctance to watch a loved one die, to quote scripture and make good an escape. Caregivers do well to pray for the courage and stamina to do God's will.

*Mother seems different today. She opens her mouth like a hungry sparrow as I shovel in her soft lunch. Her eyes glisten with innocent wonder as she stares at Dave. He watches from the foot of her bed as she gobbles down lunch. "Good to see you eating so well, Mother," he says. She chews rapidly, swallows, and says, "You look good with those feathers in your hair, George." He grins. "Thanks Mother, but my name is Dave." And of course, he wears no feathers.*

When hallucinations signal the decline of our loved one's rational mind, it is a wrenching blow to witness. It especially hurts if the loved one previously had a sharp and clear mind.

*In our case, I shovel the rest of lunch into Mother as if good nourishing food will somehow force her back to normal awareness. She jerks her head left and right, trying to see around me to her invisible visitors. "Uncle Jim! What are you doing here?" Her voice is childish with surprised joy. She claps her hands. "Hail, hail, the gang's all here!" she sings.*

When a dying parent reverts to childhood, the memories evoked may be a revelation. They give caregivers a brief glimpse into what may have been hidden before: the enthusiasm and playfulness of our loved one as a child.

*In our case, I discover my mother had a happy childhood. Even this brief visit from long dead relatives makes her clap and sing. She slides down in the bed and dozes off. Moments later, awake and rational, she orders, "Tell the nurse to give me some more of that red cough medicine."*

Mood swings from child to adult are common in certain illnesses, the professionals assure us. It is easier to accept

whatever emotional age loved ones experience upon awak-
ening rather than try to reason them into normal behavior.

> *At the nurse's station, I repeat Mother's request and add,*
> *"She seems to be hallucinating." The nurse says, "You know*
> *the patient has a brain tumor?" I nod and swallow hard.*
> *"Odd behavior will appear from now on." She pats my*
> *hand. "Just humor her."*

Good advice. Anything that caregivers do to make patients feel loved and accepted, not weird and crazy, will
ease their dying.

> *Back at Mother's room, an aide is making up her bed with*
> *clean linen. Our patient is fastened to the back of a chair*
> *with a wide belt. She is picking blackberries. Legs sprawled*
> *like a child sitting on a milk-stool, her withered fingers*
> *pluck invisible berries and drop them into a non-existent*
> *pail. We can almost hear the plunk of the berries hitting the*
> *tin bucket. We stare, mesmerized, as she fills her invisible*
> *pail. "Pie for supper," she says and smacks her lips. A*
> *childish smile flits across her face. The corners of her lips*
> *turn upward, an exaggerated happy face. Her smile comes*
> *and goes as she listens to the chatter of invisible compan-*
> *ions. The acquiescent smile is hard to watch. It is too oblig-*
> *ing, too obediently happy—a good little girl eager to please*
> *her elders.*

Wouldn't it be great to sit on a milk-stool and pick black-
berries instead of shouldering our adult responsibilities?
Caregivers may often long to be children again in our parents' house. Safe in a loved one's arms, sheltered from the
pain of the hard days ahead. Are we resentful of new duties, or is it simple self-pity?

❦

*Lord, who is that happy person reliving a childhood event? What happened between then and now to change him/her into a serious and sometimes angry person? Does he/she wish to be just a kid again, happy and carefree? Lord, did you ever wish to return to the quiet life of Nazareth? To be just Mary's son, the carpenter? To escape the sure agony of the cross? You did not shirk your assignment, Lord. Teach us now to accept your will. When we would fall victim to self-pity, help us remember all the sacrifices our loved one made for us. It is our turn to give back now. Help us, Lord. His/her shoes are too big for us to fill.*

# Chapter 12

*"Hide me in the shadow of your wings."*

*Psalm 17:8*

David, king of Israel, is persecuted by his enemies. Even the mighty warrior, who slew a giant with a pebble, seeks reassurance and protection from God.

Sometimes not only the enemy of terminal illness but a plague of well-meaning relatives beset the busy caregiver. Overwhelmed by Martha-work, we seek God's protection. *O God! Hide us from these people! We feel smothered in tea and sympathy. We need a quiet space to think and pray. Help!*

> *Out-of-town relatives arrive in droves for brunch. The small house hums with conversation. They hug and kiss and tell us what a blessing we are for our loved one. Their well-meant sympathy fails to soothe our exhaustion. Instead, the sting of easy tears encourages another bout of self-pity. Dave escorts the relatives to the hospital. I stay home to catch a quick nap.*

Caregivers must take time to rest. Even a half hour nap snatched between duties will rejuvenate us. Caring for a dying person is a grueling vocation. We need all the strength we can gather, from whatever source.

> *Later, dazed from a fitful nap, we serve high tea to a crowd of hungry relatives. The food vanishes along with gallons of*

*coffee and tea. The relatives regale us with funny tales of their childhood. Dave tells the George and his feathers story. One aunt laughs until she cries. "She was always so bright, so bright," she says, weeping over our loved one's mental deterioration.*

The easy tears of sympathetic relatives somehow make caregivers feel better. It is comforting just to know others empathize with our grief. Hugs and kisses are fine, but tears shared over our impending loss feel more healing.

*After the company leaves, we visit the hospital. Mother sleeps through supper. The food on her tray congeals as it cools. Dave drinks her coffee. We seem to be subsisting on coffee. Our nerves hum with caffeine, our thoughts scatter and drift. We have problems making the simplest decision. Instead of consulting the nurse about Mother's deep sleep, we merely sit and watch her. Mesmerized by lack of sleep and too much stress, our heads nod in time with her deep snoring.*

The passive apathy of sleep deprivation may be a warning sign to caregivers. Time to back off, take some time off, catch up on our sleep. How can we effectively take care of someone if we are too tired to think?

*My sisters, arriving for their late evening visit, chase us home to rest. But even now there are visitors, local relatives, big-eyed with worry. "Grandma is fading so fast!" Joy and Ed, Betty and Len join our son Mike and his daughter. Company fills the living room and overflows into the kitchen. Mike makes coffee, twice. No one refuses the cup of comfort.*

Caregivers may feel overwhelmed by people, by their needs for emotional support, for conversation, for coffee. We need a quiet space to sort out our raging emotions, to

think and pray in silence without having to respond to endless questions. The loved ones try to bolster us, to lend
emotional support as we face the challenges of home-care.

*In our case, we appreciate their generous hearts, but will
company time never end? And, always, the dog Ginger demands attention. Her wants are blessedly simple: food, clean
water, and daily walks. In return for meeting her needs, she
provides us with quiet comfort, a warm body under our restless hands, soft eyes full of unspoken sympathy.*

Beloved pets can be a wonderful distraction in times of
stress. They depend upon us for their daily care. Yet because they are so loyal, they will forgive a certain amount
of neglect.

*Our dog Ginger also provides comic relief. Joy assigns her-
self the job of "putting the dog outside." Ginger, house-
trained as a puppy, would rather bust than make a mess
inside. When she climbs the basement steps and whines in
the back hall, Joy assumes the dog needs to go out.
Actually, Ginger, a social animal, wants to join the crowd
of people upstairs for a round of pet-me. Joy puts Ginger
outside, and promptly forgets her. Later, when the smokers
go outside, Ginger, greatly insulted, waits in the dampen-
ing grass beside the driveway. She keeps her back turned to
the door to show her abject disapproval. Joy, abashed, tries
to soothe her. "Oh, poor Ginger," she says, trying to gain
the dog's forgiveness. But we all giggle at the dog's outraged expression. Ginger is not amused. She holds her
queenly head erect, highly insulted by this neglect. Only a
cookie, given as a peace offering, makes Ginger look at us
with favor again.*

❦

Lord, we feel besieged, shut out of your kingdom like a dog in the night. We wait for a kind word to make things right again. Send us sweet peace to soothe our troubled souls. Shelter us under the wings of your favor, O Lord of all. Grant us the courage to endure. Fortify us for the days ahead.

# Chapter 13

*"To you O Lord, I call; O my Rock, be not deaf to me...Hear the sound of my pleading, when I cry to you, lifting up my hands toward your holy shrine."*
Psalm 28:1-2

Even though he sinned greatly, King David prays that he may not be punished with the wicked. This verse from the psalms may be encouraging for caregivers. If even a great sinner like David has the courage to beg for God's help, surely God will listen to our prayers too. We may feel overwhelmed by the rapidly increasing responsibilities of caring for the terminally ill. Soon our loved one will need complete care. It will be a daunting challenge. How will we find the strength to help this loved one?

*O Lord, be my Rock!*

> *We attend a meeting with a Hospice worker in Mother's hospital room. She instructs us as to the necessary requirements for home-care—an adjustable bed, oxygen equipment, sickroom supplies, etc. All will be furnished by Hospice and billed to health insurance. "Do you have her bedroom ready yet?"*

Although loved ones may wish to die at home in their own bed, it is more practical to use a high, hospital-type bed. Much easier on the caregiver's back, for one thing.

Some dying ones wish to have their bed set up in the living room, handy to the kitchen and television set. That way they won't feel isolated from the center of family activity.

*In our case, our loved one is very ill, and a very private person. "We will have her bedroom empty and ready for your equipment tomorrow." Although we speak about her as if she cannot comprehend our words, Mother watches from the bed, alert and full of questions. "What time is it? What time?" she asks over and over.*

Sometimes it takes a caregiver a while to realize the patient's interest in the time is caused by awareness of a schedule for pain medication. It may be a mistake to dismiss all repeated questions as trivial, or mere incoherent babbling.

*In our case, our loved one needed her dose of liquid codeine. Her next question, asked while we are alone, catches me off-guard. "What do I have?" Her eyes squint with determination. I swallow a lump of fear. She nails me with the hard stare that always demanded the truth when I was a child. I couldn't fool her then. I still cannot lie effectively. "Mother..."*

The health care experts remain divided on the question of what dying people should be told. Is it better to tell them the truth about their terminal illness and risk plunging them into declining despair? Or should we sugarcoat the prognosis and pray for a miracle healing?

*In our case, we had no choice. "Tell me the* truth! *What do I have?" she demands. I gulp. "You have a tumor."*

Whoever said the truth shall make you free must have lied, at least when it comes to explaining terminal illness to a victim.

*"A tumor?" Her voice falters. The skin around her eyes, already dark and shrunken, seems to swallow up her courage. She closes her eyes. A tear trickles down her cheek. "Why? What did I ever do to deserve this?" Her despair makes me weep. "I'm sorry. You don't deserve this at all." She turns her head away. "Go away now. I want to sleep." I watch a while, unwilling to leave her alone with the demons of fear and pain. Her eyes remain closed. She fingers the red rosary wound around her wrist. Her lips move in silent prayer. Reassured, I tiptoe out, leaving her to Jesus and his Blessed Mother.*

❧

*O Lord, be our Rock. When we would despair, hear the sound of our pleading. Teach us to rely on your divine love. You know we can't do this alone. Mother of our Savior, keep our loved one in your blessed care. Give him/her the courage to face the long days of pain and fear. And, Jesus—we need lots of help too.*

# Chapter 14

*"Know that the Lord does wonders for his faithful one."*

Psalm 4:4

David, while still a young shepherd boy, often soothed the unstable King Saul with songs played on a harp. Psalm 4 is dedicated to this often depressed leader. Did David guess that down the centuries, millions of suffering souls would find comfort in his simple songs of praise and trust?

Caregivers often pray that God will send comfort and healing miracles to our loved ones. *He/she has served you well all his/her life, O Lord of all. Please hear our plea now as our loved one struggles with this illness. Heal him/her. We know that you do wonders for your faithful ones. Don't let him/her suffer the final agony. Heal him/her now!*

> *We convert her bedroom to a sickroom. A double bed is moved to the den for our use. The big dresser with its double mirror stands at the foot of the new hospital bed. When the head of the bed is raised, our loved one will be able to see her favorite family photographs lined up against the mirror. We stare around at the transformed bedroom. It is a cheerful room, bright with afternoon sunshine. Pale curtains flutter at the windows facing the backyard. Late season roses struggle to bloom one more time. The apple tree our children climbed up and fell out of is almost bare of leaves. A few for-*

*gotten apples litter the lawn. The grass looks healthy and green. It needs trimming.*

Sometimes caregivers, locked into the life and death struggle of a loved one, forget that everyday life goes on, with or without our attention or permission.

*We turn back to stare at the almost empty room. My parents slept here for the forty plus years of their marriage. My siblings and I were conceived and born here. Whenever we were sick enough for the doctor to visit, we always waited in our parents' bed for his kind attention. Mother suffered through countless miscarriages and two stillborn babies in this bedroom. Now we are surprised at how small the room is to have contained so much family drama. Soon it will play host to the grand finale of her life. This room will see her dying. I shudder at the thought and flee the room.*

Moments like these, when caregivers ponder memories of times past, may act as emotional milestones. Which do we really want to remember, the happy times or the sad? We also need to find acceptance of the here and now. It is too emotionally taxing to constantly battle against the reality of approaching death.

*That evening our youngest son telephones from California. He is uneasy because of a troubling dream. "I dreamed you died, Mom," he says, his voice shaking. "It's not my time to die, Jim. I am needed here to take care of Grandma." He is not reassured. "But you sound funny, Mom. Are you all right?"*

Caught between the duties of caregiving and the sometimes endless responsibilities of our own families, how can we be all right? We endure, we pray, the Lord does wonders for us.

*In our case, our son senses something physically wrong. His concern makes me smile. This is the child we feared would never survive his childhood asthma. Now he is a big strapping man giving his mother orders. "Do you have a sore throat? Go see a doctor." I agree. "Okay, first thing tomorrow."*

❧

*Lord, when we would succumb to self-pity, remind us of how often you have blessed us. Thank you for loving relatives concerned about our well-being. This must be a way you do wonders for your faithful ones. You send ordinary people with generous hearts to come to our aid. Remind us to be always grateful for the miracle of family love. Keep us faithful to you, Lord.*

# Chapter 15

*"Stay in the one house eating and drinking what they have, for the laborer is worth his wage."*

Luke 10:7

Jesus gives instructions to his disciples as they begin their first missionary journeys. These ordinary men were very brave to go out and spread Jesus' revolutionary teachings about peace and brotherly love. This happened even before their controversial messiah died and rose from the dead. They must have often felt unwelcome, yet they persevered.

Caregivers sometimes feel unwelcome in their loved one's home. Their good intentions may be misinterpreted as nosy interference.

> *In our case, we feel like interlopers in my mother's house, sorting through her private belongings. It is a labor of love on our part, yet we feel unworthy.* Poor children, over-worked, unpaid, unwelcomed by the mother of the house. *We pray to overcome self-pity, for that is what it really is.*

It is difficult, under any circumstances, to finally release favorite grudges that should have been resolved and forgiven years ago. Under the pressure of a fatal illness, we must forgive now before the chance for reconciliation is gone forever. The loved one we so often thought of as our perpetual enemy will soon be gone. That loved one needs us now. This is the only important thing. We must labor to make home a welcoming place for our loved one.

> *My son was right about my sore throat. A noon appointment at a clinic sends me home with antibiotics for an infection. Exhausted, I nap while Dave and a Hospice worker set up the new hospital bed. When I awaken, dazed and confused from my medication, the sight of that clinical bed sends chills down my spine. Its metal side-rails look like prison bars to me. "Mother will hate it," I tell Dave in a weepy voice. He hugs me. "She didn't seem to mind the bed at the hospital, and this one is the same, right?"*

Caregivers may find it so difficult to accept the reality of a loved one's approaching death. We indulge in magical thinking. If the bedroom remains the same, then our loved one will not change either. We delude ourselves that if only we keep everything from changing, our loved one will not die.

> *In our case, we rebel against her familiar bedroom now transformed into a sickroom bristling with strange furniture and oxygen equipment. My eyes mist over. Dave breaks into my mournful thoughts. "We need to shop for soft foods for Mother. Do you have any money?" I shake my head. "You?" He turns out his pockets and grins ruefully. "I'll call Joy." My sister, the family banker, advises us to take money out of Mother's purse for groceries. We gasp at the very idea. "Don't be silly, Sis! Mother has to eat and so do you two. It would cost far more if we had to hire a nurse to care for Mom."*

The seeds of unworthiness are rooted in childhood. Some of us are slow to weed out the tangle of unnecessary parental dependence.

*My heart pounds with childish guilt as we slip money out of Mother's purse. As children, and even into adulthood, none of us were allowed to touch her purse. Now we feel like sneak-thieves. But Jesus said, "The laborer is worth his hire." Isn't that what we are now—servants doing the Master's work, caring for the sick?*

❧

*Lord, teach us how to be your humble servants. Strengthen us when childhood hangups try to sabotage our labors. This is a tough job, Lord. We need to put aside foolish inadequacies and concentrate on the real needs of our loved one. Teach us, Lord, how to be blessings for our loved one, not sniveling children, hampered by old memories, helpless to make him/her comfortable.*

# Chapter 16

*"Be on guard, therefore. The Son of Man will come when you least expect him."*

*Luke 12:40*

Jesus tells his followers to always be prepared for the master's return, even if he comes "like a thief in the night." A primary lesson for Christians is to keep our spiritual houses in order. We must always be prepared for the final coming.

· This scripture verse may speak to caregivers preparing for the return of loved ones from the hospital. They are the masters of the house. Everything must be made ready for their final journey home. The night before, caregivers may sleep uneasily. Dread of the heavy responsibilities keeps us tossing and turning. We listen for the telephone to ring. Do our subconscious minds actually *want* a phone call announcing death and letting us off the hook? Like fish in a net, we twist and fight the nightmare.

> *In our case, we wake up late and rush to the hospital. Mother is excited about going home. Propped up in bed, she picks at her breakfast tray. Globs of scrambled eggs scatter down her bib. Her hands shake as she attempts to navigate a spoonful of stewed fruit from tray to mouth. Encouraged by her tiny appetite and determined efforts, we sit and watch. She tires quickly and sinks back against the pillows. "Can you help me drink the coffee?" Her voice trembles.*

Caregivers may waste energy grieving over every new sign of weakness in our dying one.

> *To me, the fact that my mother can no longer hold her own coffee cup seems like a major blow. I hold the thick mug to her lips. She takes a long noisy swallow. Suddenly she is choking. I rub her back and wait for her coughing to ease. Mother coughs and chokes. Her face darkens with her efforts to breathe. Her lips turn blue. I run for the nurse. The coughing changes to a croup-like whoop. Mother sounds very like our Jim when he almost died of asthma.*

Now our concern becomes focused where it should be, on vital health needs, not on the insignificant act of steadying a coffee cup for our loved one.

> *We wait in the hall while lung specialists work over Mother. We listen as her choking gasps for breath go on and on. Dave hurries down the hall to telephone Joy and Ed. When they arrive, their gray faces reflect the fear we all feel. Is this it, the day we lose our mother?*

During a crisis, all the silly stuff falls away. Like frightened children, caregivers and family lock together in terrible unity. They cling together. They wait.

> *Betty and Len arrive an hour later, their faces etched with fear. "Are we too late?" Betty asks. She stands near the closed door to Mother's room and listens to the harsh sounds from within. Her shoulders shake. "She can't die, yet. She just can't!" Len gives me a fierce hug. "You have always been the strong one in the family, Sis," he says. "Keep your chin up. We need your strength now."*

Caregivers may be assigned a role as "the strong one" when they don't feel strong at all. Whether they accept the role thrust on them is a personal choice. Often it is a struggle not to throw themselves down, beat their fists against a closed door, and wail.

> *As if tuned in to my churning thoughts, a nurse opens the door. "You can come in now and stay with her. She won't be going home today." We wonder which home the nurse means, Mother's house, or her heavenly home? We are afraid to ask. It is enough to be allowed to stand beside her bed and hold her icy fingers. She seems even more shrunken, diminished by the choking spell and her desperate struggle for each breath. A full oxygen mask hides her gray lips and flaring nostrils. Only her eyes, the haunted eyes of a trapped animal, are visible. They blink rapidly, tearing as the equipment roars around her bed. She is very frightened.*

A near-death experience may be terrifying, not only for the victim but for the family. Though we think we are ready for the death of our loved one, a close call teaches us otherwise.

> *The afternoon wanes into early evening. Technicians monitor her progress. Her lungs are steamed twice to ease her labored breathing. She clings to the oxygen mask as a drowning victim clings to a lifeline. The hours drag past in agonies of fear, ours and hers. She is afraid to die. We are afraid to let her die. As daylight fades, her breathing grows more quiet.*
>
> *At 8:30 p.m. the nurse sends us home. We all linger over our goodbyes. We wonder if this will be the last time we will see Mother alive.*

❧

*Lord, whenever you approach, teach us to be ready to welcome you with open arms. Watch over our loved one* and keep him/her in the shadow of your loving care. Even if you come for him/her like a thief in the night, please don't let our loved one die all alone and afraid. Banish fear. Bless him/her with peace and comfort when you call his/her name. Comfort us also in our fear. Teach us to welcome the master's return.

# Chapter 17

*"Fear is useless; what is needed is trust and her life will be spared."*

Luke 8:50

Jesus is called to the house of Jairus to cure the ruler's daughter. On the way, crowds slow Jesus' progress. Someone tells Jairus his daughter is already dead, but Jesus continues to the house. He cures her, one of many healing miracles in the Bible. For caregivers, the key scripture verse is: "Trust and her life will be spared." Do we dare seek such a healing miracle for our loved one? Do we trust enough to put that precious life in God's hands? Relinquishing all control to the Lord means we must accept his decisions. What if God decides it is time to take our loved one home to heaven? Sometimes our childish hearts rebel at the thought. *No! Don't take him/her yet. We are not ready to let go.*

> *Mother is better this morning, but the hospital won't send her home until next week. She sleeps peacefully as we visit, her lunch untouched. We watch for a while, our hearts thumping with gratitude for her easy breathing, then go home.*

Why are we mere mortals so afraid of relinquishing our loved ones to the Father's care? Surely heaven is a grander place than this flawed earth. People never really die, scripture tells us, they merely pass through the veil of death and into the arms of Jesus. Yet, we mortals are so afraid of death. It is still the great mystery, this unknown step to eternity.

> *A rainstorm brings a flood of water to the basement floor. It refuses to drain away. We call in a plumber. He offers a practical solution to the flooded basement, a sump-pump. Joy, the family treasurer, agrees to have the work done. She wants it done Monday, but we stall her off. "Mother will be coming home next week. It will upset her to have strange men working in her house."*

Even the dying are entitled to peace and quiet. Why plan major home improvement projects when a loved one, especially a lifelong frugal person, will certainly object?

> *"And you know what she would say?" Joy laughs. "Mother would say, 'You can't even wait until I'm dead to start spending my money!'" Standing in the partially flooded basement, we giggle together. Our exhaustion and relief at the near-miss yesterday makes us giddy. Accusing whines from outside catch our attention. The dog stands outside the basement window in the rain. Ginger's pelt is soaked, her ears dripping. Her eyes accuse us of gross neglect. She stares down at us, the bedraggled victim of our absent-minded distraction. "Oh, poor Ginger," Joy says. We laugh so hard, we feel dizzy. Joy stumbles up the stairway to call in the dog. Ginger will not look at us, any of us, especially as we continue to howl with laughter at her outrage.*

Caregivers know how good it feels to let go once in a while. Far better stress escapes as insane laughter than as hysterical weeping. We must never be afraid to rejoice even in a house of death. Trust in the Lord will help to soothe our aching hearts.

❦

*Lord, when we would perish from anticipation of sorrow, remind us of your many blessings. Thank you for funny pets and giggling family members. Teach us to trust in your mercy, Lord of all. For you alone know what is best for us.*

# Chapter 18

*"Have pity on me, O Lord, for I am languishing;*
*heal me O Lord, for my body is in terror; my soul,*
*too, is utterly terrified; but you,*
*O Lord, how long?"*

Psalm 6:3-4

Psalm 6 is the first of the penitential psalms. In his affliction, David begs God for mercy, praying he will be saved
from death. It should be comforting to know that even a
great king feared death. Yet, we all still fear the final unknown. What will really happen when our loved one
makes that terrifying step over the threshold of life into
death? We cling to God, through the promises of Jesus
Christ, asking him to soothe our fretful souls.

> *Mother seems quiet this morning, a Sunday. "A nun*
> *brought me communion," she says. "I was anointed, too."*
> *Her forehead wrinkles above the ever-present oxygen mask.*
> *Her dark eyes bore into mine. "What do I have?" she de-*
> *mands. I wonder if she remembers asking the same question*
> *three days ago. Maybe she is hoping for a better answer this*
> *time. Unfortunately, my answer has not changed. "You*
> *have a tumor, Mother."*

Accepting the approaching death of loved ones is difficult
for caregivers. We fight, we deny, we grieve. Yet, eventually,

we accept our loss and go on living. For the dying ones, the hope of going on is limited by the uncertain mysteries of life after death. If they do not trust in God's mercy, they may cling tenaciously to life in this world.

> *In our case, the negative answer to our loved one's question wounds her just as much the second time. "But will I get better?" The glitter of hope in her sunken eyes makes my stomach churn. Why must I always be the bearer of bad news? Choked by grief, I shake my head. The hopeful glitter fades away. "I'm sorry, Mother," I whisper and touch her hand. She draws away from my touch. "I'm sorry, too." She closes her eyes, shutting me out of her pain. A tiny tear trickles down her cheek. She refuses her lunch, turning her face to the wall and feigning sleep.*

Sometimes we may wonder if loved ones blame us for their illness. Possibly. It is easier and safer to blame someone close, like a family member, for an inexplicable tragedy, rather than to rampage against God.

> *Dave hugs me out of the room. We attend our granddaughter Stephanie's birthday party. She is a joy to watch as she totters around the legs of relatives. Her other grandparents, several aunts and uncles, all fill Mike's apartment with cheerful conversation. Dave goes outside to "talk cars" with our sons.*

Caregivers, even those well supported by family ties, need happy times, times of renewal. When possible, attend those parties. Be grateful for the chance to relax and forget, for a little while, the difficult times ahead.

> *Stephie holds up her arms to me. I hug her wiry little body and drink in the warm wiggly feel of her. Something Mother told me pops into my mind. During my grandmother's fu-*

*neral, Mother's little sister was only five. "Children are a comfort at a funeral," she told me. "All those tall uncles would bend over and pick up Gertie just to give her a hug. It helped them, you see, to know that life goes on, even after the death of their beloved sister."*

Remembering the wisdom of the ages passed down from parent to child is a comfort as the time of parting draws near.

*I hug Stephanie and put her down. She gives me an echo of Mother's shy smile.*

❧

*Lord, when we are afraid, comfort us. Remind us that life does not really end at death, it is just changed. Teach us to rely on your mercy, O Lord of creation. Save us from the terrors of our own imaginations.*

# Chapter 19

*"The Lord said... Will we have arguing with the Almighty by the critic? Let him who would correct God give answer!"*

*Job 40:1-2*

Job, the afflicted servant of God, asks why he must suffer. The Lord's answer is sharp. In effect, "Who do you think you are, questioning the Creator?" The lesson is clear. God has his own reasons for allowing pain and suffering in the world.

Caregivers may not be ready to accept the Lord's will. Like Job, our human nature stirs us to question and argue. *Lord, why are you doing this? Why did you allow our loved one to suffer that most dreadful and painful of diseases? Why couldn't you have taken our loved one peacefully and saved all of us so much pain?*

> *In our case, our prayer/argument brings no peace, only another restless night. The dream terrors grow fierce as the approach of the homecoming draws near. We awaken groggy and cranky, reluctant to face another day.*

Caregivers, displaced from familiar routines, may often wish the "problem" of caring for a dying one would just vanish. Wouldn't it be great if all this was just a bad dream?

It seems difficult to square our shoulders for the emotional challenges ahead.

> *Mother seems bright today, hungry, but too weak to feed herself. She polishes off half the food on her tray, then turns away from the spoon. "No more." I pick up a warm wash- cloth. She screws up her face like a toddler and dodges the cloth. It makes me grin to see this familiar reaction in an adult. "You look like Stephie, squirming away from the washcloth."*

It may be a major mistake to treat an adult like a child. Even a helpless dying person has dignity.

> *"I can wash my own face!" she retorts. "I'm not that help- less." I hand her the cloth and wait while she swipes at her lips. After a moment, she wipes carefully at her eyes. "Have they been putting your eyedrops in, Mother?" She shakes her head.*
> *"I'll get the nurse," Dave says.*
> *"Never mind," Mother says quickly. "I'll be home tomorrow. We can do it then."*
> *Dave, never one to accept orders from Mother, leaves the room. Her fists pound the sheet. "Why won't he ever listen to me?"*

The invalids' feeling of helplessness increases as their strength decreases. Strong-willed people do not change when they fall ill, they just shout their orders louder from the sickbed.

> *I attempt to smooth away her agitation. "He's just stubborn, like you, Mother." She snorts. "Can't wait until I start get- ting my strength back. I'll show that hard-head who's boss." My smile fades. If only Mother could get her strength back!*

*If only she could rally enough to defeat the devil devouring her from within. My eyes sting with forlorn hope. O God! Can't you spare her this last indignity?*

Do other caregivers have this running argument/prayer with God? We echo Job, pleading with the Almighty for our loved one's cure.

*"What are you standing there crying about?" Her harsh voice jerks me away from my inner squabble. I shake my head and turn away from her scathing glare. She thinks tears are a sign of moral weakness. I am shaken and confused by the return of her normally tart tongue. She pounces. "Tell me the truth this time! What do I have?" My tears overflow. Does she think I would lie about her sickness? Could I be that cruel? "Will I get better? Answer me!" She grabs me with surprising strength. "Tell me the truth. Now!"*

Caregivers are not the only ones to argue with the Almighty. Our dying loved one may try any tactic to change the terrible prognosis, even bullying the caregiver.

*I shake my head and back away. "You know the truth, Mother. Yelling at me won't change anything." She sinks back into her pillows, panting. Her eyes are wild. They roll from side to side like a trapped animal searching for escape. Her harsh breathing roars through the room. I try to replace the oxygen mask on her face. She bats at my hands. "Go away! Leave me alone to die!"*

The vocation of caregiving is never easy. But once we are committed, even a major guilt trip inflicted by our loved one will not deter us from our duties.

*Dave and the nurse appear in the doorway and quiet Mother's ranting. She turns her back on all of us. The nurse motions us to leave. We escape. Dave says, "Are you going to be able to take care of her without nurses to smooth off her rough edges? Will it be too much for you?" I square my shoulders. "If you help me."*

The moral support of others is so important to caregivers, especially when dealing with a difficult patient.

*"It won't be easy. My mother really gets mean when she is crossed." Dave grins. "Tell me about it." Like Simon of Cyrene, he will help carry our cross to Calvary and beyond.*

🌰

*Lord, fighting with our loved one is almost like quarreling with you. It is a no-win situation. O Creator, when we would brace ourselves to do battle with you, teach us instead to accept your will without question. For no one ever won an argument with the Almighty.*

# Chapter 20

*"Go home to your family and make it clear to them how much the Lord in his mercy has done for you."*
*Mark 5:19*

Jesus drives out a legion of unclean spirits from a man living on the other side of the lake. The healed man tries to join Jesus in the boat. Jesus knows this man will serve God better by being his witness to the surrounding cities. He sends the man home.

Scripture does not reveal the reaction of the man's family. We may wonder if the former wild man, who had lived in the tombs screaming and gashing himself with stones, was welcomed home. Or did his arrival cause feelings of love and anxiety? Caregivers may empathize with that frightened family as we bring our loved one home.

> *Mother arrives in an ambulance. Attendants gently lift her onto a wheeled stretcher before opening the side door of the house. She looks pale and shrunken beneath the thin hospital blanket. Sun in the brilliant blue sky peeks between puffy white clouds. She shivers and shuts her eyes against the brightness.*

Dying people turn ever inward as their time approaches. Even what may be a last glimpse of bright sky and clouds may fail to interest them.

*Attendants carry her up the steps, through the hallway, and into the bedroom she has occupied for sixty years. The short trip from hospital to home exhausts her.*

Caregivers may also feel exhausted from emotional tension at the homecoming of our dying one. The transfer of responsibility for the patient's care, from the professionals in a hospital setting into the home-care system, may fall heavy on our shoulders. The what-ifs plague us: What if our loved one shrieks in pain? What if we can't help? What if…? But the realities of caregiving are seldom as traumatic as our imagination would have us believe.

*Mother sleeps all afternoon and wakes up hungry. She is mild as milk and relieved to be home. No tantrums today. My heart swells with gratitude to have her home, and, at least for now, happy.*

Rejoice and be glad for what the Lord in his mercy has done for us. Every happy moment needs to be cherished, hoarded away in our hearts to warm us during the chill of the bad times.

*That evening, we have long telephone conversations with family in California. One of our sons mailed us money to "tide us over." "God bless your generosity, Tom," Dave says. We are blessed with family. Who cares if we are poor, money-wise? Family love brings enduring riches.*

❧

*Lord, thank you for blessing us with family love freely expressed. Sorrow shared is so much lighter a burden. Let your name be always on our lips and in our hearts. Teach us to count our many blessings, instead of ranting and raving against your crosses. In Jesus' name, Amen.*

# Chapter 21

*"The cords of the nether world enmeshed me, the snares of death overtook me. In my distress I called upon the Lord and cried out to my God. From his temple he heard my voice, and my cry reached his ears."*

Psalm 18:6-7

David sings to the Lord after his rescue from enemies. Like the ancient warrior king, caregivers may feel enmeshed by the snares of death. Our loved one's acute needs wrap around our days like a smothering vine. We may feel panicked, choked by the fear of doing the wrong thing and causing more pain. In our distress, we call upon the Lord for strength.

*Lord, help! Our loved one is so needy right now. Help us to do the right things to ease the pain. No more arguments, Lord. We know that only you have the power over life and death. We ask only that you make us patient and kind.*

> *After giving Mother her pain medicine with a tiny amount of liquid breakfast, I mix up bread. She has always loved the smell of freshly baked bread. She accepts a milksop lunch (soft buttered bread soaked in warm milk). Her eyes search my face as I help her eat. She touches my hand lightly, a gesture of affection.*

Even so slight a gesture from our dying loved one should be cherished, and remembered.

> *Len arrives bearing gifts. He is loaning us his blender for milkshakes. He also brings a large schoolmarm's bell. "That way you can ring when you need something." Mother accepts the bell warily, rings a single clear note, and drops it. "Too loud."*

For a suffering person, even a sharp sound may bring acute pain.

> *Her eyes blink sleepily. "Nap time," she says. I lower the electric bed into a gentle recline. She needs her head elevated in order to breathe better. The oxygen mask helps too. A doctor from Hospice arrives and examines Mother. In the living room, she puts our minds at ease about the patient's death. "She won't choke the way she did in the hospital. She will drift into an oxygen-starved coma, and finally just stop breathing."*

To a frightened caregiver, a coma sounds so easy, so peaceful. Maybe the death of our loved one won't be so painful after all. We take a deep relieved breath for the first time in days.

> *Outside Ed and Dave come back from a lumber shop with supplies to fix the rotting floor of the porch. The sound of their busy industry broken by occasional laughter soothes me into an afternoon nap.*

Primary caregivers are usually women. While our nursing duties keep us constantly busy, men in the family need work too.

*In our case, fixing up the neglected house keeps the guys busy. At 3:30, Mother knocks the bell off the bedside table and jerks me awake. "You rang?" I say, a parody of a television character. She does not smile at my feeble joke. Intense pain makes her arms and legs tremble. Greedily, she drinks a double dose of codeine. Her pain does not ease. The fierce grip of her hands betrays a depth of agony.*

Unrelenting pain means we need help from the professionals.

*Hospice telephones a prescription to their pharmacy. The guys race through heavy suburban traffic to fetch the painkiller. I read the label and my heart sinks.* Morphine. *Mother doesn't care what the label says, she craves relief. At 7:30 p.m. she finally relaxes into an uneasy sleep.*

Caregivers are often frightened over the reality of loved ones' severe pain. A bottle of liquid morphine seems too flimsy a weapon against unrelenting agony. What will tomorrow bring? Will they be able to eat anything? We feel the cords of their pain wrapping tight around our days. Our lives will be governed by their needs from now on. The uneasy thoughts frighten us.

*At bedtime, I give Mother her medicine, check her diaper, and arrange the oxygen mask. She seems content. Her eyes blink sleepily. I turn off the lamp and tiptoe out. The bed springs squeak as I ease off my robe and stretch out. She calls out. I leap up and fumble into my robe. Mother thrashes around on her bed. I turn on the lamp and check the time. Too soon for more morphine. She is calm again. Her eyes twitch in REM sleep. Did she have a drug-induced nightmare? I wait a while, then turn off the lamp. She cries out. Turning on the lamp seems to end her agitation. I sit*

beside her bed and wait. After an hour of watching her
peaceful sleep, I leave her dresser lamp turned on and stag-
ger back to bed. It is 2:00 a.m. At 5:30 she calls for her pain
medication. She smiles, pleased at herself. "I slept all night."

❦

Lord, grant us the strength to care for our loved one. It
is so hard to see him/her helpless and in so much pain.
Help us to serve well. Teach us to forget personal fear and
sleepless nights. The cords of the nether world cannot en-
mesh us as long as you are by our side. As the snares of
death overtake our loved one, let all we do for him/her be
in your name, Lord Jesus.

# Chapter 22

*"Whoever wishes to be my follower must deny himself, take up his cross each day and follow in my steps."*

Luke 9:23

Jesus instructs his disciples that sacrifices will be necessary if we wish to follow him.

Caregivers know that all roles in life call for sacrifices. But we may find sleepless nights and sickbed vigils a wrenching sacrifice. The invalid must be lifted from bed to chair so bedding can be changed. A smooth bed is important. The sick person may spend most days in the same favored position. A small red mark on hip, elbow or spine signals the beginning of a bedsore.

> *"Bedsores are no fun, Mother." She shrugs, a limp lifting of her bony shoulders. She is so wobbly, we must hold her upright in the chair. Mother slumps, breathing deeply into her oxygen mask. Her hair looks straggly, her eyes, desperate. "Can't you hurry up?" she says querulously. "I need my cough medicine."*

The disintegration of staunch adults into querulous children who beg for medicine is often a blow to caregivers. We want them to be stronger than we are, not a weak whining invalid. What happened to those adults who would rather bite their tongue than admit they need anything?

*My shaking hands fumble the bed linen smooth. We lift her back into bed. She slumps against the pillows with a gasp of relief. I give her liquid morphine and the oxygen mask. Her eyes slam shut. She sleeps.*

What do caregivers do while a loved one sleeps? After laundry, cooking, and praying, what's left to pacify churning thoughts?

*I sit beside Mother's bed. Spread across my lap is a favorite yellow blanket with a torn binding. Bursts of occasional sunshine flood the cheerful color of the blanket as I sew the satin ribbon. The needle flashes in and out. It is soothing to sit thus, sewing up sunshine. I can forget for a while the reason for my duties here. Mother's hoarse voice startles me. "You don't have to sit there and wait for me to die. This may take some time, you know."*

The frank words of invalids are sometimes unintentionally funny. Other times, deliberate gallows humor takes over the sickroom.

*The needle jabs my finger. I hurry from the room. On my return, she is asleep on her side, facing the far wall. Her diapered bottom hangs outside the sheet. When I cover her, she awakens and rolls toward me. Her eyes, blurred from the potent drug, stare at my face. "Mother?" she says. Her wide incredulous smile breaks my heart.*

When a dying person slips through the cracks of reality, caregivers assume new roles, often a parent to our parent.

*"Go back to sleep, Elvie," I say, using her nickname from childhood. She stares long at my face as if memorizing it. "I'm sick, Mother," she says, and rolls away to face the wall. I swallow the lump in my throat and pat her shoulder until she snores again. I feel privileged to have witnessed the blissful expression on Mother's face. She loved her mother very much.*

Humoring our dying loved one has many rewards. Visiting past relationships between long dead family members is a thrill.

*When Joy and Ed visit, Mother is unable to see either of them. Joy squeezes between the bed and the wall. "Here I am, mom. Can you see me now?" She takes Mother's hand and glances up, worried. "Her right eye looks funny, kind of cloudy." I shrug helplessly. Maybe the brain tumor? I mouth. Joy reads my lips. Her face trembles. She pats Mother's hand briskly.*

How deep is the thrust of approaching blindness for our loved one. When that person cannot recognize us, it cuts through our good intentions like a knife.

*Mother turns her milky vision toward me. "I need cough medicine," she says. After I give the morphine, she closes her eyes in weary relief. I fasten the oxygen mask. Joy and I watch her fall asleep. My sister's lips tremble. "She's fading fast! She doesn't act like Mother anymore."*

Caring for even a cranky loved one is somehow easier than the indifference of the new stranger in our loved one's room.

*After lunch, I crash in the den bed and sleep until after 5 p.m. Mother is puffing with pain as I hurry to fetch her morphine. "Why didn't you call me, Mother? I'm just in the next room." She grits her teeth. "You needed your rest." Again she is a thoughtful parent suffering in silence rather than calling for help.*

❦

*Jesus, help us accept this heavy cross. It is so difficult to watch his/her decline. He/she has always been so strong and tough, larger than life. Now, step by step, he/she is dwindling before our eyes. We feel daunted by new roles as parent to our parent. Lord, help us endure this cross without falling into self-pity. Teach us to live each day with profound gratitude for the time he/she has left. And thank you, Jesus, for this opportunity to serve you by serving him/her.*

# Chapter 23

*"Why is light given to the toilers, and life to the bitter in spirit?"*

Job 3:20

Job, the upright man of the Old Testament, longs for death. Even his shrewish wife torments him. She urges him to curse God and die. Satan wants Job's pure soul. God believes Job will overcome the devil's curses and remain innocent. Job complains and wishes for death, but he also endures.

Caregivers may empathize with Job's torment as we watch our loved one in agony. The *Why God?* question boils up within us like a festering bedsore. *Why did you allow our loved one to contract that terrible disease? Why must the innocent suffer? Why, God? Will we ever know the answer?* Thankfully, we have little time for long arguments with the Almighty. Our loved one's needs are too pressing. The pain medication may not really make them comfortable. Instead, it transforms them into strangers. We never know who they will be when we approach the sickbed. Will they be patient Job or shrewish woman?

> *Today, Mother is her normal stoic self. We delay her mid-morning morphine dose because a Hospice nurse is due at 10 a.m. Maybe they will change her dosage. Mother's frequent forays into childhood worry us. Are we contributing*

*to her confusion by giving too much painkiller? Nurse Jean soothes us with practical common sense. "The patient should be on a regular schedule of meds, every four to six hours, to prevent pain. The hallucinations may not be the morphine. Don't forget she has brain tumors."*

In every fatal illness, some aspect is particularly hard for caregivers to accept. It may be the loss of strength in our loved one, the gradual eroding of mental capacities, or a loathsome (to us) physical symptom.

*In our case, we did not want to lose any last vestige of our loved one's adult personality. Caring for her was difficult enough. When she regressed to childhood, it seemed even harder to take. Her whimpers of pain, sounding like our own children's cries during their illnesses, sear our hearts.*

God knows what he is doing when he puts women in charge of children and invalids. He gives us hearts of wax to melt with compassion.

*Nurse Jean takes us into the living room to discuss the future. "Have you and your sisters made the final arrangements yet?" At our blank expressions, she continues. "You know, pick a mortuary and a coffin?" I shake my head numbly. The very thought of "making arrangements" for Mother's funeral chills my soul.*

What is there about this routine question, usually asked by Hospice workers, that makes caregivers so uneasy? Is it hitting the wall of our own denial? The question shakes us up, makes us live in reality time. No more magical thinking. No more wishful pretending that our loved one will recover. No more if only...*He/she is going to die!* We need to make plans for a funeral.

*Some families find it a comfort to have everything set up ahead of time. In our case, we are not ready for that step yet. When I call Joy and ask about making final arrangements, she is not ready either. "Let's play it by ear, okay, sis?" Neither of us wants to even think about this part of the future, let alone make concrete plans for Mother's funeral. Maybe later, but not now.*

☙

*O Lord, help us to face the reality of our loved one's approaching death. We are like frightened children, afraid some naughtiness of ours will cause us to lose our parents. Enlighten us, O Lord. Help us believe that death is not a punishment, but the beginning of eternal reward for a life well lived.*

# Chapter 24

*"They wait for death and it comes not; they search
for it rather than for hidden treasures."*

*Job 3:21*

Job, weary of suffering, is impatient to die. He cannot understand why God allows him to live in agony, when his very soul cries out for deliverance. Caregivers, weary of watching their loved one suffer, may also wonder as they wait.

*In our case, we wait for a delivery from the Hospice pharmacy. After that first trip across town for medication, new drugs are delivered. The nurse requested enzyme patches for the worsening bedsore.*

Making the dying patient as comfortable as possible is the main thrust of the Hospice Program.

*Mother flinches as I press on the patch. Her arms fling out in an infant's "startle reflex." She moans.*
*"I'm sorry, Mumma." My use of a childish endearment surprises both of us. She has been the stiff title, "Mother," for too many years. Now reduced to helpless neediness after so many years of staunch independence, her pain softens me into childish adoration, again.*

Part of the pain/pleasure of caring for a dying relative is the chance, the *last* chance, to mend fractured relationships.

*Mother calls out in a loud voice. "The girls! I'm sick and I can't take care of the girls!" She throws aside the sheet as if to rise and plunge into mothering chores. "Betty! Jocelyn! Where are you?" I press her down again. "Don't worry, Mother. I'll take care of the girls." She sinks back against the pillows and gives me a long searching glance. "I'll leave everything in your capable hands, Cecile." As I pat her shoulder until she relaxes into sleep, I feel like laughing and crying at the same time. Mother is relying on me to "take care of the girls." Obviously she is replaying scenes from the past when she spent time in bed after her many miscarriages. The day-to-day care of my sisters, born less than two years apart, must have been a major worry to her then. I wonder how her tangled thoughts came to believe that I was caregiver in those days. My sisters were eight and six when I was born.*

Maybe God assigns all of us to be caregivers, regardless of time or place. Didn't Jesus say, "Love one another"?

*I smooth the bedcovers and adjust mother's oxygen mask. "I'll leave everything in your capable hands." My eyes sting. It is the nicest thing she said to me in years.*

Why do parents and adult children have so much trouble expressing love for each other? Are we too much alike, bristling with such tough shells of self-righteous pride that love can't penetrate either way? How wonderful it would be if we all could simply say, "I love you," without fearing the whiplash of rejection.

*In the afternoon, Mother awakens shouting, "The baby! Where's my baby boy?" She will not calm down until I slip a folded sofa pillow between her thrashing arms. "Here you go, Mother. Shhh! He's sleeping." She quiets immediately. She cuddles her "baby." The pillow/baby is our brother, Jim, the miracle child of her middle years. He died years ago. I stare at the large crucifix above Mother's bed and blink back scalding tears.* Soon they will be together again, Lord. United in death.

Slowly, God's will for our loved one invades our rebellious hearts. We almost accept the inevitable. Our loved one will certainly die. *But not yet, Lord. Not yet, please!*

*In the evening, Mother's mellow mood evaporates. She glares and turns away from the spoon. "Come on, Mother. You must eat something to keep up your strength." The word is spat out between compressed lips, "Why?" I stare at her, speechless. Why indeed? I offer another spoonful. She shoves my hand aside. "This is no life for me. Why are you trying to prolong my agony?" Her eyes glitter with rage. I glance at the clock. Two more hours before morphine. "Are you in pain, Mother?" She makes an impatient sound. "I'm always in pain!"*

When pain is pervasive, call Hospice for a stronger medicine.

*"I want to die!" Her voice is hoarse. I turn from the doorway, trying to smooth the horror from my face. Eyes squeezed shut, her lips move. A favorite rosary marches through bony fingers. "Good-bye. I'm going now!" She rips the oxygen mask off.*

Caregivers may watch, horrified, as loved ones try to stop breathing by sheer power of will. Usually painkillers take over and they fall into a drugged sleep. Our hearts pound, a reaction to surges of adrenaline. We wait and watch. We wonder if a strong death-wish will outrace eroding disease.

*All night long, Mother shouts and mumbles and wrestles with death. I am afraid to sleep in case she needs me.*

❦

*Lord, why does he/she have to suffer the indignity of this helplessness and pain? It tears us apart to see him/her like this, so needy, crying out in unbearable agony. Why prolong his/her bitter life in endless suffering? Take him/her, Lord. He/she is ready to die.*

# Chapter 25

*"I waste away; I cannot live forever; let me alone,
for my days are but a breath."*

Job 7:16

Job pleads to God to let him die. Even this upright man grew weary of pain and begged for relief.

For caregivers, watching our loved one's body slowly disintegrate, the scripture verse takes on personal meaning. As we witness the acute suffering, it transforms our prayers for a miracle healing into pleas for a merciful death.

> *During the night Mother shoves her mask away. Because the liquid oxygen produces a thin mist, the bed coverings are soaked. Her pajamas stick to her heaving chest. Her haunted eyes, dark pools of pain, blink up at me. "Am I dead yet?" I swallow hard and resist a familiar urge to make light of her blunt words. Mother will not look kindly upon any attempt to humor her this dank morning. I peel off her sodden clothing. Her face wrinkles in disgust as she peeks at her naked chest. I wonder if the sight of her now sallow skin offends her modesty, or if it is lost pride in her once stately body that makes her say "Pah!"*

Sometimes caregivers to the elderly are surprised at the strong remnants of pride that still cling to our loved ones.

They mourn for lost youth, for the waning strength of withered bodies.

> *Mother has always been broad of shoulder and hip, well padded with muscle and flesh. Now reduced to skin over bones, her sallow skin pulls tautly over jutting bones. The sore on the base of her spine is worse. The edges of the enzyme patch look raw as it weeps blood.*

Dear Jesus, how your mother must have mourned as your bloody body hung on the cross! Teach us compassion, Lord.

> *In the evening, the sisters visit. Betty has not seen Mother since last weekend. She is shocked. "You're so skinny, Mother," she says. "Aren't they feeding you?" Betty turns to me. Her gaze is reproachful. I squirm, scalded by her implied criticism. "Mother refuses to eat." Betty says, "She will eat for me." Her winning ways coax tiny bites of nourishment into Mother.*

Although a caregiver may be grateful for a sibling's power over a difficult parent, we still feel furious at both of them. Reduced to pouting children, outsmarted and outmaneuvered, we jockey for favor at our loved one's bedside.

> *I stomp out of the bedroom to join the others in the living room. Joy pats my arm. "Don't let them get to you, Sis. We both know Mother can be difficult, right?" I nod agreement and feel better. The sisters and their husbands do not stay long. We are grateful for the return to a peaceful house.*

Caregivers may find it difficult sometimes to tread the fine line between adult and childhood relationships. No matter how mature we wish to be, all of us still strive to be our parent's favorite child.

*The peaceful house doesn't last long. Two of our sons drop in for coffee and a bargaining session down in the basement. Dave sorts the tools and lawn equipment into separate piles. The guys speak for their choices. I watch for a while, happy our sons will glean some benefit from their grandfather's vast collection of junk. But when their voices grow loud as they haggle over a favorite item, I retreat upstairs. It is too much for me, this dispersing of possessions. It comes too close, in my fertile imagination, to the tossing of dice for Jesus' cloak as he hung on the cross.*

Most families wait until after a loved one's death before they wrangle over possessions. Some dying people, aware of their limited days, prefer to give away their possessions beforehand so they can appreciate the gratitude of the survivors.

*To drown out the bickering voices in the basement, I turn on the oxygen machine and strap the mask over mother's face. Her eyes blink sleepily. I smooth hair away from her face. It feels sticky, oily. "Tomorrow we'll wash your hair, Mother." She glances up. "Good trick," she says tartly. "I can't even get out of bed." I grin at her spunk. This is the mother I know and love. "I'll just drag in the garden hose." The mask fogs up as she snorts a hollow-sounding laugh. The brief movement sends spasms of pain through her body. Desperation beads her forehead. Time for morphine again. It is past midnight before she falls, gasping, into uneasy sleep.*

🖤

*O Lord, ease our loved one's struggles. He/she wastes away before our very eyes. And while he/she suffers untold agony with every breath, we find ourselves reduced to* petty jealousy of more favored siblings. Forgive us for our childishness. Keep reminding us that nothing matters except making our loved one's final days more comfortable. Let there be no room in our hearts for quarreling and selfishness now. He/she needs us too much. Help us be warm and loving, not cold and judging. In Jesus' name, Amen.

# Chapter 26

*"How long, O Lord? Will you utterly forget me?
How long will you hide your face from me? How
long shall I harbor sorrow in my soul, grief in my
heart day after day?"*

*Psalm 13:2-3*

Oppressed by foes, forced to hide in caves to insure his safety, David laments his desolation and prays for God's help.

The sickroom of a loved one may feel as dark and oppressed as David's caves as the enemy draws ever nearer. Every day is a battle against ongoing agony and our swelling grief. Like the psalmist, we find ourselves praying, *O Lord, how long?*

> *Mother has a restless night. She awakens moaning and thrashing at 1:30, 3:30, 5:30 and 7:30 a.m. As Dave eats breakfast, I leave for morning mass. He wants me to drive to conserve my energy. I feel the need to walk for fresh air and exercise.*

Caregivers find their own pattern to reduce stress.

> *In our case, my husband kept busy fixing up the old house. He worked off stress in sweat equity. I used fresh air and ex-*

ercise. *Twice a day, one walked the dog, the other did the dishes.*

Some caregivers knit or do crossword puzzles. Others obliterate stress by reading the Bible or watching TV. And, of course, we all pray.

*The cold morning air burns my lungs with brief freedom. I pray for strength. It is the hardest thing I have ever done, watching my mother slowly die. Her increasing agony tears me apart. Back home, Dave leaves for church. I begin Mother's bath. She seems stronger this morning. Her body feels firm as I roll her from side to side. She stares at me as I squeeze a small bottle of watered down shampoo onto her hair. Bubbles foam as I massage her dry scalp. A warm damp washcloth removes the grimy suds. She closes her eyes as I dry her thin white hair. As I gently drag a comb through her hair, she grabs my wrist. Did I hurt her?*

When loved ones suffer so much pain, caregivers are almost afraid to touch them for fear of doing more harm than good.

*"Listen to me!" Her voice is stern, a mother giving an order to an always obedient child. "I want you to kill me!" The comb slips through my fingers. "You heard me! Do it now, before he comes back." I pull away from her fierce grip on my arm. "You must be joking, Mother. I can't kill you." Her voice grows louder, more desperate. "You can and you will!"*

Nothing prepares a caregiver for this agonizing moment. Not only does our loved one wish to die, we are *ordered* to make it happen.

*I back away, shaking my head. She tries to sit up but falls back weakly. Her voice is not weak. She shouts at me. "Don't you understand? I want to DIE!"*

Most caregivers were taught to honor mothers and fathers, to be obedient to their every command, regardless. But how can they actually carry out parents' orders to *murder* them?

*Chills run up and down my arms. This must be a bad dream. Mother, always a devout and pious woman, would never ask such a thing of me. "Kill you, Mother? No. I can't do it." Her voice deepens to a hoarse scream. "Yes, you will! Take me out. TAKE ME OUT!"*

The horror of the death wish intensifies as our loved one pulls out all the emotional stops. To a dying person in agony, nothing is sacred, not personal ties, nor the Ten Commandments.

*Dave stands in the doorway, his forehead wrinkled. He stares at Mother. "What's going on? I heard your shouting clear out in the driveway." She is howling now, her chin pointing to the ceiling like a demented animal. "TAKE ME OUT! TAKE ME OUT!" Dave's voice is calmness itself. "Take you out where, Mother? To a fish-fry?" The queen is not amused. If looks could kill, we would both be dead-meat now. She raves, "Put me out of my misery. Now!" The raw hate on her face stings my soul. I look away. "Don't turn away from me! I gave you an order. Now do it! Kill me!"*

What answer can we give when our loved one demands the ultimate obedience? Which is more important, obeying a dying person's direct command to effect a release from agony, or obeying the law of God and man: Thou shalt not kill?

*"Don't you understand?" she roars. "I WANT TO DIE! YOU HAVE TO KILL ME! I INSIST!" She thrashes on the bed. Spittle sprays from her lips. I have to scream above her shrieking. "NO! I won't kill you! You should be ashamed to even suggest it. You want to go to hell?" I touch the rosary on her wrist. Her face grows livid. She unwraps the rosary and flings it at the wall. "Hell?" she shouts. "I'm living in hell right now!"*

❦

*Lord, how long will you torment our loved one with such dreadful agony? Have you utterly forgotten him/her? Day by day the pain marches on, increasing in strength as he/she writhes on the deathbed. He/she must be in unspeakable agony to ask us to kill him/her. Our hearts, trained to be obedient, melt before this acute suffering. But when we would weaken and even consider his/her pleas for a quick merciful death, remind us that we are not you. You have the power over life and death. Not us. But, O Lord, how long?*

# Chapter 27

*"Howl, for the day of the Lord is near...."*

Isaiah 13:6

Isaiah, a prophet, comforted the Israelites during their captivity. He often used the phrase, "the day of the Lord," to signify the future coming of the Lord in power and majesty to inaugurate his kingdom. The phrase was meant to give hope to the captives and strike fear in their captors.

Caregivers often feel like captives in the sickroom. We are bound by duty and love to preserve our loved one's life, even when that person howls, "I want to die! You have to kill me!"

> *Our loved one refuses to take no for an answer. Dave turns me toward the bedroom door. "Leave her alone for a while. She'll calm down when she loses her audience." Mother continues to rant and rave. Every hate-filled word roaring from the bedroom seems to set up an answering echo in my head. "Die! Die! DIE!"*

Caregivers sometimes wonder: Why aren't we bold enough to put them out of this misery? Other adult children have faced the same challenge, as we know from reading the media splashes about euthanasia. Other victims of terminal illnesses have been quietly killed at their own request, with little fuss and few legal repercussions. But murder is still murder. *Thou shalt not kill.*

*Mother's howls continue for another hour until she falls into a groaning sleep. When I approach her with noon medication, she bats the spoon away untasted. "Okay," I say on a deep indrawn breath. "Let me know when you need your pain medication." I wonder how long she will rage at me, at life, at God. I am tempted to press a pillow over her twisted face if only to still the hate-filled words. "If you loved me, you would kill me." I can live with that statement, but the next one brings me to my knees, blubbering. "You are useless!"*

Why do we allow the ranting and raving of terminally ill persons to affect us? Surely it is pain speaking, not their real hearts.

*Dave slams her bedroom door. He gathers me in and hugs me tight. "She doesn't mean those hateful words. It's the brain tumor talking, not your real mother."*
*I believe it is my real mother talking. "No. She means it, Dave."*
*He says, "Don't listen to her." His hug calms me.*

Caregivers must cling together, especially when we are sorely tempted to perform a mercy killing. The Lord will strengthen us.

*As we cling together, Joy and Ed walk in the back door. She stares at my tears. "What? Is she dead?"*
*Dave quickly releases me. I swipe at my eyes and try for a laugh. "Mother is in a rage. She…"*
*Dave says, "Mother told us to kill her. She pitched a fit when we refused."*

*Joy sags with relief. She marches up the stairway. Her lips are tight. Joy takes it as a personal insult that our mother wants to die. My sister battles every day to survive. Now Mother wants to just give up!*

Each victim of terminal illness reacts differently. Some people give up without a fight. Others battle to the last drawn breath.

*"I'll speak to her," Joy says. Behind the bedroom door, loud voices echo in fierce argument. I join the men in the kitchen. Ed makes coffee. We wolf down sandwiches.*

During times of severe stress, many caregivers (and others!) turn into stress eaters. We feel so empty inside. Food soothes us.

*A weary Joy joins us. Her gray face reflects a battle fought hard and lost. "Mother is on a tangent. She won't listen to reason." Ed makes a mild joke. "So what else is new?" We share a family laugh. We all know from hard experience just how difficult Mother can be. From the bedroom comes the sound of unearthly howls. They set up hungry echoes in our empty hearts. We dive into the food.*

❦

*O Lord, feed our empty hearts with the good food of your salvation. Teach us to trust in you while the howls of our loved one surround us. He/she is only human, Lord, a pitiful creature who needs your loving hand to sustain him/her. He/she wants us to help put him/her to death. We are tempted, Lord, to shove him/her through the gates of glory into your loving arms. Help us with this, our temptation to play God.*

# Chapter 28

*"Do not be concerned for your life... or for your body, what you are to wear."*

Luke 12:22

Jesus tells his disciples not to worry about earthly things because the Father knows (and will provide) such things.

Caregivers, living on faith as we care for our dying ones, may forget this message about total trust in the Father's will.

> *At lunch, Joy stares at my face. "You need a break, Sis. Will you go shopping with me? I need a dress for—well, you know." I did know. We both need dresses for the upcoming funeral. Our mother's funeral. We just can't say funeral out loud, yet. Ed gives Dave a long look. They both nod at some secret communication between them. "Go shopping, ladies," Ed says. "We'll take care of Mother," Dave says, "if she'll let us."*

For a primary caregiver, just getting out of the house is a treat. We have been too busy to notice that the sun still shines. Deep breaths of cool fresh air taste wonderful. Thirsty for freedom, we try to drink enough of this rare air to last forever.

> *Joy chatters away as she drives to the nearest shopping mall. She is a dedicated shop-till-you-drop bargain hunter. I*

*don't like shopping—too many choices, never enough
money. Joy finds a lovely two-piece dress that fits her per-
fectly. Nothing fits me. I am soft and flabby from too much
stress food and not enough walking. The sight of my bulky
body in the dressing room mirror disgusts me. Price tags
alarm me. I cannot justify buying anything new for me.
I'm not worth it. Mother's words keep echoing in my mind.
You're useless!*

Why do we allow hurtful words, shouted in extreme
pain, to shatter our sense of self-worth? Is it because a
loved one shouted? Or because we somehow believe we
deserve the hateful words? Caregivers must come to terms
with inner guilt (we all harbor inner guilt!) over unresolved
quarrels or troubled relationships. We need to love ourselves more.

*We leave the mall. Joy carries her new dress. I am empty-
handed. We pick up fried chicken for a late supper and go
back to Mother's house. Betty and Len and our son Mike
share supper with us. Betty frowns at me across the crowded
table. "Why isn't Mother's oxygen turned on?" I stiffen at
the implied reproach in her voice. "Because she just shoves it
away, that's why!"*

Caregivers, uncertain of whether we are helping or
hurting our loved ones, often bristle at the slightest hint of
criticism.

*Joy glances from one sister to the other. It is a family trait
that our faces reflect every mood. I am furious at Betty for
questioning my nursing skills. She is insulted because I
snapped at her. Joy says, "Mother won't eat or take her medicine, either." Betty gloats, "She took medicine from me." I
shove away from the table. "Great!" I say tightly. "Can you*

*come every three or four hours and get her to take her pain
meds? Sure would save me a lot of hassles." Betty's face
pales. "Oh, I can't. I have to work." We remember how glad
she was to escape Mother's care when we arrived three
weeks ago.*

It is so futile to engage in sibling rivalry. Caregivers need
the loving support of all family members. Why waste energy bickering?

*I bite my tongue now before it blurts out more trouble. Joy
shoots me a sympathetic glance. "The important thing is
that Mother did take her pain medicine." I nod agreement.
Beside me, our son Mike lets out a long sigh. He had been
watching the tense interplay between sisters with a worried
frown. Now the tension eases. I give him a warm smile and
hug his arm.*
*"I'll come over every day, Mom," he says, a promise he
keeps. After supper Mike volunteers to do up the dishes, "so
Mom can rest." Gratefully, I hit the bed for a nap.*

Sometimes all it takes to clear the air is a frank discus-
sion of the caregiver's needs. No one will help if we don't
ask.

*When I awaken, the company is gone and Mother is
screaming again. "Take me! Take me!" she howls to the ceiling. I wonder if the neighbors will call the police and report
elder-abuse. She does accept her morphine, even though she
refuses to look at me. Fine with me. I don't want to look at
her angry face, either. After a half-hour of torturous
screaming, she falls asleep. My head pounds with tension
and guilt.*

O Father, we want to trust in your will for our lives. Teach us not to quarrel with family members. Comfort our aching hearts when our loved ones shout at us. They do not mean the hateful words. Yet, even if everyone on earth is angry with us, you still love us. Don't forget us, O Lord, as we travel through the valley of death with our loved ones. Strengthen us. Teach us that your love is enough for us, now and forever.

# Chapter 29

*"Remember that my life is like the wind; I shall not see happiness again."*

Job 7:7

Job's friends, in the discussions that make up the book of Job, insist that God is punishing him for personal wrongdoing. Their self-righteous arguments for Job's repentance add to his depression. An innocent man, he wants only to escape misery.

Caregivers empathize with Job and their loved ones in their seemingly endless trial of agony. Our hearts ache for the victims so helpless, so determined to die on their own terms. It may be a pride thing, we realize. They, fiercely independent, seek final control over their days. As Job's friends were, we are caught in the middle between God and his suffering servant.

*Mother is quiet this morning after the usual restless night. She opens her mouth for the liquid morphine, drinks it like a starving child, then turns away. She is giving me "the silent treatment." I hide a rueful smile of recognition. So that's where I learned that sly trick of control. I pat Mother's shoulder. When she stiffens and jerks away, I know she is not catatonic as she pretends to be. She refuses to even consider food.*

A change in the patient's attitude toward food signals a time to call Hospice and report on the latest challenges.

> *My description of Mother's rage to die brings a lovely visiting nun to the house. She gives mother a particle of host. I hold my breath as the morsel reappears on her lower lip. Will she reject even our Lord? Sister Jude gently pushes the host back into Mother's mouth. She finally swallows. The nun and I release breath in a shared sigh.*

If dying persons will still accept sacraments, it is a sign that they still believe in God's mercy. A ray of hope!

> *Out in the living room, Sister Jude speaks to us for a long time. Her gentle words strengthen us. "Your mother loves God very much. She is so anxious to be with him, she can't wait. It won't be long now. Keep praying for the strength to care for her. I'll pray for you, too."*

The prayers of others strengthen beleaguered caregivers. Don't be afraid to ask for these prayers.

> *Joy and Ed come over to a meeting with nurse Jean. She reassures us that Mother's death-wish is not unusual, "especially in elderly people who have lived independent lives. They want to keep control over their lives, and deaths. It's very hard for them to accept their new helplessness."*

Knowing that heartache is shared with countless others may help caregivers a little.

In our case, it does nothing to ease our loved one's agitation. When the nurse bends over to listen to her heart, Mother takes a swing at her! The nurse backs away, calm in the face of obvious rejection. She grins a little.

*"Spunky, aren't you?" she says. Mother snorts and turns away. "Make sure she drinks enough liquids so she won't become dehydrated."*

When a loved one refuses all food and drink. Hospice provides a gadget, a tiny sponge on the end of a round stick.

*"Dip the sponge in water, then rub her lips with it. Enough moisture will trickle down her throat to keep her going." Keep her going? For what? Why would Mother want to keep going any longer than she has to?*

As assigned caregivers, we accept the sponge on a stick and use it whenever the patient allows us—which may not be very often.

*In the afternoon, a priest visits to anoint mother. We stand at the bedside and join him. She stares at us, her mouth agape, her eyes dull. Father uses holy oil to trace the sign of the cross on her forehead, the palms of her hands, the tops of her feet. I pray that she will not kick out at him. Placidly, she accepts everything without rebellion. We recite the Lord's Prayer to complete the ritual. Mother's hoarse voice surprises all of us. "Give me communion!" she bellows.*

How strong the faith of our dying ones can be. They crave the outward signs of faith more than food or water.

*In the living room, Father Bob says, "I took care of my father during his last days. Attending to the needs of the dying can be very beautiful."*

Caregivers may have little patience for platitudes. Beautiful? Are we missing something along the way? What can be beautiful about the wracking pain, the wasting away, the actual disintegration of a strong person into helpless agony? What can be wonderful about listening to that person scream for death? We pray for enlightenment.

❧

*Lord Jesus, this is so hard! Help us see your loving hand in all this misery. Like Job, we wonder if we will ever see happiness again. Will this nightmare never end? We need your strength, Lord, the strength you showed on Calvary as you accepted death on the cross for us. Help us endure, O Lord!*

# Chapter 30

*"I solemnly assure you, you shall see the sky opened
and the angels of God ascending and
descending...."*

*John 1:51*

As Jesus gathers his disciples, some of them are surprised
that the humble carpenter's son has such amazing abilities.
Jesus tells them, in effect, "You haven't seen anything yet!"

Many people believe in angels, those winged heavenly
beings assigned to watch over us. At the deathbed, caregivers often report feeling the brush of invisible wings.

> *Mother mumbles off and on all night. She accepts the pain
> meds, the dampened sponge, but nothing else. She is deterio-
> rating before our eyes. Her mouth hangs open. When we try
> to gently close it, her neck and jaw are stiff. Precious
> painkiller, liquid morphine, dribbles down her chin. I give
> her extra to make sure she gets enough. By midmorning, she
> is catching angels.*

What other explanation is possible for a loved one's
weird behavior? This person, propped up by pillows,
watches invisible beings flying over the bed. The eyes,
dark and filmy, shift slowly from side to side, tracking the
angels flying past just out of reach, the mouth agape in as-

tonishment. One hand reaches out to catch the visions. The fingers open and close. Is our loved one touching the face of God?

> *I hasten to wrap Mother's rosary around the side rail of the bed where she can easily touch it. Her seeking fingers close into a fist. She drops her hand and falls into a deep sleep. I stand and stare at her wasted face. It is like looking at a stranger. All familiar contours of her body, the peach-soft face, the strong life-force that gleamed from her eyes, all has changed. Her body is skin over bones, her face gray and lined. Her shadowed eyes are closed, shutting me out. Where is my feisty mother? Will she die before she forgives me for disobeying her last (shouted) wish?*

As death approaches, many people believe God sends angels to welcome his own. It is an eerie sight to witness.

> *A Hospice social worker drops by at noon. She encourages us to use the Respite program.*

Hospice maintains beds in nursing-care facilities or hospitals for respite care. The dying person is admitted to the facility for a few days. This allows families who feel overwhelmed by the care of their dying loved one to take a few days off. The chance to catch up on much needed rest, to even sleep all night for a change, sounds wonderful.

> *In our case, we remember how exhausted Mother felt after her brief trip home from the hospital a week ago. She is weaker now. The ambulance trip would be too traumatic for her.*

No matter how difficult it may be to care for a loved one, we do not want that person to die among strangers.

*In the afternoon, Joy stares at Mother's emaciated face. She picks up one limp hand and squeezes it. Tears roll down my sister's face. "Mother is so skinny! She looks like a prisoner of war." We weep together. "She is a prisoner of war."*

❧

*O Lord, watch over and protect our loved one as he/she enters the valley of death. Send your angels to keep watch over him/her lest he/she stumble. Calm our frightened souls, Lord, as you draw ever nearer. Teach us to rejoice, not to mourn, as he/she journeys into your loving arms.*

# Chapter 31

*"He will bid his angels to take care of you."*
*Matthew 4:6*

During the temptation of Jesus in the desert, the devil taunted Christ with verses from Psalm 91. Even the tempter recognizes the power of angels.

Caregivers begin to welcome these invisible unearthly beings as our loved ones slowly slip away.

> *That afternoon after the others leave, I fasten Mother's oxygen mask. She does not fight me this time. By supper time, her breathing changes to short heaving gasps. Her eyes are half open. She stares at nothing. No angels flying tonight. I miss them. She allows me to hold her hand. It feels limp, a cold lifeless claw. Above the oxygen mask, her forehead gleams with sweat. Thin hair sticks to her scalp.*

A drastic change in the patient's condition calls for a gathering of family members.

> *Joy arrives, takes one horrified look, then calls Hospice. Nurse Jean sounds surprised. "I didn't expect...so soon. Keep me posted," she says. "Call anytime day or night."*

Hospice teaches us: Don't call 911; call Hospice. Ambulance attendants are required by law to use heroic means to revive dying people. Caregivers do not want loved ones to suffer any longer than they have to. That is, most family members do not want them to linger on.

*In our case, Betty is the exception. She arrives pale and hysterical. She grabs mother's limp hand and sobs, "You can't die! You can't!" There is a slight response from Mother. She turns from her staring contemplation of the far wall and gazes blindly at Betty. The gruesome appearance of Mother's blind eye triggers shrill babbling from my sister. "Tell me you love me! You can't die until you tell me you love me!"*

Why is it so difficult for some people to let go of a dying loved one? Surely heaven is preferable to an agony of earthly pain?

*Mother rallies. A mumbled reply hissing through the oxygen mask sounds like nothing resembling human speech. Yet Betty sinks back on the chair, comforted somehow by this brief response. I am outraged at my sister's selfishness. Why can't she let Mother die in peace? Why drag her back from the sweet relief of Jesus' arms? I leave the bedroom to sulk in the living room. Maybe it is jealousy at Betty's power over Mother that sparks my outrage?* Mumma's favorite.

The sickroom may play host to life dramas as varied and colorful as life itself. As soon as we realize what our various reactions mean, we may feel ashamed. A deathbed is no place to play out a petty sibling's game. The family should be united in grief, not torn apart by old resentments.

*Yet my anger at Betty does not abate. Maybe it is easier, and safer, to be mad at my sister than to rage at God. My sister will forgive me because she loves me.* But what will God do to me?

A lapse into sibling jealousy may trigger an additional childish emotion, fear of God. Instead of the loving heavenly Father who has been a daily comfort throughout our adult lives, our personal vision of God may revert to the frightening God of early childhood. We are afraid to rage at this all-powerful Creator of heaven and earth. Too risky. But what to do with our churning anger? An annoying sibling makes a handy target. Small wonder, we think, that families quarrel when death strikes down a loved one. *We have to blame someone, God.*

> *I say a quick prayer to banish my childhood demons of jealousy and fear, and return to the sickroom. Betty accepts my brief hug. Through her silky blouse, her bones feel like antique china ready to shatter.*

During a deathwatch, the house often fills with relatives. If caregivers waste their time bickering, they may miss the final significant hours of a loved one's life.

> *Mother's body is shaken by several seizures. Her eyes bug out. Fingers splay, hands clutching the air. Her feet thrash against the sheets. The sound of her harsh breathing permeates every corner of the house.*

When the deathwatch grows intense, some caregivers must find an escape.

> *I go outside and stand in the frozen night air. I stare up at the beauty of the brilliant stars, wishing Mother could see the stars tonight, so beautiful, so bright. I wonder, as the brightness of her life dwindles away here on earth, if a heavenly star will grow in beauty when she dies. I think about "catching angels." I pray that angels will come. Soon. Ginger whines, her nose pressed against my hand. Her wise*

old eyes glow crimson in the dark. We both shiver and go inside to resume the deathwatch.

❦

*Lord, our loved one's family is gathered now to witness your ultimate power over life and death. Grant him/her peace and comfort in these final hours. Will you open the sky for him/her? Send your angels to welcome him/her to your heavenly home. Console our aching hearts. And, Lord, teach us patience with family members!*

# Chapter 32

*"Do not let your hearts be troubled. Have faith in God and faith in me."*

John 14:1

Jesus seeks to give comfort and strength to his disciples. He is about to be arrested and put to death. His followers suffer an agony of fear and grief.

Families and caregivers suffer that same fear and grief as angels hover ever nearer to their loved one.

> *My sisters and their husbands share the deathwatch with us until 1:30 a.m. Then Betty makes an excuse for leaving. We hug her goodbye.*

As the life of a loved one draws to an end, some family members find it too painful to watch. Why waste energy arguing? The patient's condition will not change no matter what we say. Still, it is difficult to think charitably, to make excuses for the escape. Some people suffer an acute dread of the final sorrow. But their leaving, when a loved one's death is so near, still feels like desertion. *"Could you not watch…with me?"* Jesus asked his disciples in the garden of Gethsemane.

> *At 2:00 a.m. Joy collapses on the couch. Dave sleeps upstairs and I crash in the den. Ed remains awake, watching and waiting.*

"Watch and pray that you do not enter into temptation."

*Mother has an epileptic seizure during the night, but at dawn she is still with us. Ed rubs his eyes and asks for coffee. Joy struggles up from her tangle of blankets. Pale and hollow-eyed, she doesn't ask about Mother. No need. We all hear her tortured breathing.*

The sonorous breathing of a dying loved one echoes the dread in our hearts. Caregivers find themselves counting each gasp, wondering when or if the torturous sounds will ever cease.

*"Stay there, Joy. I'll bring you coffee." She sinks back onto the couch with a long sigh. "How can you take it, Sis?" she asks. "Listening to that oxygen machine day after day would drive me nuts!" I hand her a cup of coffee. "It won't be forever." Joy bursts into noisy sobs, then dries her eyes. "How is Ed doing?" she says. "Ready for a break. We'll take over now."*

He found them sleeping, for they were exhausted from sorrow.

Caregivers, to protect their own health, often alternate the deathwatch. It is too stressful for family members to watch and wait both day and night. Taking turns at the bedside makes sense.

*Nurse Jean surveys mother's condition, noting she can no longer swallow even water. She phones in new meds and shows us how to insert them into mother's rectum.*

Why is it so difficult to perform the intimate duties required for the care of a dying person? Is it false pride/

shame? Are we daunted by the mere thought of touching a loved one's most private parts? God created our beautiful bodies. If we pray, he will grant us the power to overcome our personal aversions. We can then do what needs to be done to alleviate the deep pain.

> *Ed and Dave take up positions at Mother's head and feet. They are afraid she will kick the capsules out of my shaking hands. But she lies very still, her eyes squeezed shut against this latest indignity. She voices no protest as the suppositories slide deep into her intestinal tract. We pray that she realizes we are trying to help her, not torture her.*

"Do not let your hearts be troubled. Have faith in God and me."

> *Late in the afternoon, Joy makes an appointment at the funeral parlor. What was unthinkable a few days ago now assumes the utmost urgency. We hurry out to make final arrangements. Exhausted, worried that Mother might die before we get back, we rush through the choices of coffin and other services.*

Caregivers may react to this duty with unusual behavior. A sudden burst of singing, or cracking jokes, is not uncommon. All the emotional tension, the serious talk about death arrangements, must be alleviated in some way, even if in uncontrolled silliness. We may hug each other and laugh until tears come.

> *That evening, Betty watches Mother's tortured struggle for each breath. Betty does not attempt to touch her. She seems too quiet, almost as catatonic as Mother.*

As death draws near, some people withdraw from the

painful scene, a way of becoming resigned to the approaching death. Caregivers pray, for everyone's sake, that there will be no more hysterical pleading, no calling the loved one back from the edge of peace.

> *After everyone leaves, I stand at the bedside wishing for a final sign of love. Grief swells my heart as I remember how she raged at me when I refused to kill her. Too late now to reconcile our quarrel. I almost wish that I had the courage to do her bidding.*

How powerful are troubled apron strings tugging at our hearts! Would we forfeit our souls to secure a parent's love? Shake aside these dangerous thoughts. Only God has power to decide life and death. To be servants of the sick is our role. Nothing more.

❧

*Lord, comfort us through these last difficult days. Ease our troubled hearts. Let our thoughts be calm. Teach us to accept your will and remain your humble servants. We can't do it without you. Help us, Lord Jesus.*

# Chapter 33

*"O Lord! How long? Have pity on your servants.
Fill us at daybreak with your kindness."*
                                          *Psalm 90:13-14*

The meditation in Psalm 90 on the brevity and misery of life seems fitting as our loved one's frail earthly body turns to dust. At night we pray that God will take pity on his servant and morning will find the struggles finally ended. At daybreak the loved one is still miserably alive, whimpering for relief.

> *My dreamless sleep shatters at 7 a.m. I leap out of bed, aware that it has been seven hours since Mother's last pain meds. Each gasp for breath ends in a whimper of pain. My hands shake as I assemble suppositories. How could I sleep so deeply while in the next room she moans in pain? Her eyes are wild, her hands clutch her heaving chest. She makes no protest as the blessed pain relievers slide into her body. It seems forever before her grunts of pain change to sonorous gasps.*

No matter how good your intentions, a caregiver's body is only human. Abuse it with sleep deprivation and/or emotional exhaustion, and it will betray you by demanding sleep. For your loved one's sake, take care of your health needs too.

*Joy takes me to the bank as she transfers money from Mother's old savings account to a new account. She is afraid the bank will freeze the old account, and she will be unable to draw out enough money to cover the funeral expenses. I feel very uncomfortable witnessing this banking business. It is all necessary, but it seems cold and calculating. I am glad Mother cannot see us dipping into her savings. My heart feels hollow, hungry for the safe comfort of the past when she did her own banking and hid bankbooks from prying eyes.*

The money part of death and dying is often uncomfortable to caregivers. To us, our loved one is a pearl beyond price. Arranging to pay for the death expenses seems to cheapen the person's worth. Surely, they are worth more than mere dollars and cents. Yet, bills must be paid, including funeral costs.

*"Ready to go shopping, Sis?" I will never be ready to go shopping, but we go anyway. This time, due to Joy's persistence, we find a lightweight suit for me.*

Sometimes caregivers, hampered by a sense of personal non-worth, avoid buying needed clothing for the funeral. We give honor to our dead loved ones when we look our best for the final goodbye.

*We return home for noon meds. Mother seems dull and apathetic today. In an attempt to rouse her from a drugged stupor, I display my new suit for her approval. She stares at the rich colors, her eyes bleak. A flicker of recognition—"A new dress? How becoming!"—soon fades from her eyes. Does she realize my pretty outfit is for her funeral? Reading my thoughts, she gives a slight nod and drifts off into morphine dreams.*

As the end of life draws near, the victim of a terminal disease may mercifully slip into a coma. Bright colors, a loud noise, a familiar voice may break through briefly, but for most purposes our loved one is halfway to heaven. *Come, Lord Jesus.*

> *Mother is suffering much more today. Her restless sleep is often broken by groans. She shoves the oxygen mask aside so many times, I take the hint and turn the noisy machine off. In the sudden silence, her breathing seems twice as loud. It roars through the house, a constant reminder of her struggle to breathe. She gets morphine every four hours. Maybe she needs more pain relief?*

Caregivers, disturbed by the sounds of agony, might seek more pain relief for the patient. We want the moaning to stop. If the nurse says the dosage is right for now, we wonder how she knows how much is enough. She is not the one grunting in pain, struggling for each labored breath. Sometimes we are strongly tempted to over-medicate to ease our own conscience. But habits of obedience to authority hamper us. Reluctantly we agree to stick to the schedule.

> *"But she is suffering so much! I wish God would take her out of this misery." Nurse Jean hesitates, judging my mood, then plunges on. "Your mother may be clinging to life because no one has given her permission to let go." I snort. "Mother has never needed my permission for anything!" Jean says, "Yes, but your sister begged her not to die, right? Just think about it, okay?"*

Giving dying persons "permission to die" sounds silly. God will take them when their time is up, right? How can we possibly tell them to die? Too cold. Too heartless. But yet…

*Mother is going downhill so rapidly, it frightens us. No longer the familiar feisty person who battled us just days ago, she lies inert, waiting for relief. Her emaciated body rolls limply on the side. We insert the medication. She heaves a long grateful sigh. Ugly bedsores make us shudder. The professionals tell us that no painkiller known can relieve the deep agony of bedsores.*

*I cover Mother gently and linger beside her. I struggle to blurt out the difficult words. "It's okay, Mother. You can let go now. Daddy and Jimbo are waiting for you." No flicker of response from the suffering woman.*

❦

*O Lord, how long? He/she suffers so much agony. Have pity on him/her! We are exhausted waiting for the mercy of death. Release your servants from this bondage of endless vigilance. Please be kind and take him/her soon.*

# Chapter 34

*"You shall not fear the terror of the night nor the arrow that flies by day. Not the pestilence that roams in darkness nor the devastating plague at noon."*

*Psalm 91:5-6*

Using metaphors, the psalmist extols the benefits of trusting in God. It comes from a group of psalms (90 to 106) subtitled, "God's Eternity and Man's Frailty." The ancient followers of God often suffered terror, war, and plague. They learned that peace of mind and heart comes only from God.

> *As Mother's pestilence slowly claims her life, my sleep is haunted by nightmares. Even though I gave her "permission" to die, the child within cries out for the safe comfort of my Mother's arms. It is my turn to let go. But, dear Lord, it is so difficult to say goodbye!*

How do our dying loved ones sense our reluctance to let go? Just as parents know when their child is in trouble, so do our dying loved ones somehow read our hearts. Is this bond of parent/child neediness the last to be severed? Does it last through eternity?

> *A long day of pain for Mother. She is beginning to skip breaths. Whenever we notice a sudden silence, we race into*

*her bedroom and watch her chest. Sometimes it seems as if it will never rise again. But soon, with a snore-like inhalation, she gasps for breath again.*

The skipping breaths' symptom is a sure sign that death is near.

*Dave stays alert to Mother's needs as I catch a nap. Through the walls of our adjoining bedrooms, I count her shuddering breaths. Suddenly it is too much. That is not just an old woman dying in the next room, it is my own beloved mother. My eyes flood with tears. I weep and weep, inconsolable, a motherless child in a cruel adult world. Exhausted sleep is haunted by visions of emptiness, a barren wilderness peopled with bleached bones. A pause in Mother's breathing jerks me awake, sweating and terrified. Time for afternoon meds.*

Why are caregivers so afraid of losing our loved ones? We watch their suffering, and even pray that God will release them. Why then does the approaching death fill us with terror? We know that they will be in a better place. Yet, we are afraid.

*I find the lower plate of her false teeth on her pillow. She would be mortified if she knew. I place the lower plate in her pink cup and add water. Maybe she will want it later? Yeah! Right. I choke back tears at this new evidence of her impending death. In her real life, she would rather die than be caught without her teeth in place. But this is her real life now. She doesn't even notice the absence of her plate.*

Caregivers wonder why people think dying is beautiful when it often means the end of personal modesty and dignity. Think of death's opposite, the birth of new life. Both occasions seem neither dignified nor especially modest. We wonder if the Creator is telling us something. That we are just poor helpless critters, and that any futile attempt at personal modesty is just our sinful pride struggling for un-attainable dignity.

> *Again the house overflows with company. Betty is strangely quiet. She does not sit with Mother very long. Instead, she and Len spend a lot of time outside, smoking. Len complains because Dave will not allow them to smoke inside. "Your silly rules are making Betty sick! It's cold outside. She'll catch pneumonia." Dave is adamant. "You both know about the oxygen machine. You want to blow Mother up?" They leave in a huff.*

"Smite the shepherd and the sheep will be scattered," Jesus said. Tempers flare as the deathwatch wears us down. People are only human, after all. We can only take so much. Still it leaves a bad taste when siblings squabble over trifles.

> *Joy watches this heated exchange between Dave and Len. She gives Ed a long meaningful glance. He nods. Joy touches my arm. "Tomorrow, you and Dave get the day off. Go spend some time with your grandkids. We will stay with Mother. Just leave instructions about her medication sched-ule." We smile with relief. A day off!*

❦

*Lord of heaven and earth, sustain us when we fear the terror of the night. Keep us alert to our loved one's needs. This bitter plague makes him/her so helpless now, Lord. Teach us to trust in your goodness and mercy. Comfort us when we are fearful, for only in your arms will we find peace and courage.*

# Chapter 35

*"For to his angels he has given command about you, that they guard you in all your ways. Upon their hands they shall bear you up."*

*Psalm 91:11-12*

These scripture verses were quoted by Satan to tempt Christ to throw himself off the parapet of the temple to prove he is truly the Son of God. Jesus refused. The lesson is that the promise of God's protection will not hold true if we put ourselves unnecessarily into danger. By accepting total responsibility for our loved one's comfort and care, we may turn ourselves into martyrs. We may even try to blackmail God into doing our will. The wise people from Hospice know what they are doing when they suggest respite care for daily caregivers. Without a break to recharge our batteries, the constant deathbed watch may become too much for us. We slide dangerously close to despair, bundles of emotional wreckage nearly as helpless as our dying loved ones.

*In our case, my sister's generous offer to care for Mother today is a heaven-sent blessing. They arrive midmorning. Dave and I, giddy as teenagers skipping school, make good our escape. We drive to the country to visit our daughter and her children. They welcome us with hugs and kisses and a million questions. We admire their school work, and the neatness of their bedrooms. "We cleaned for three hours, Grandma!" Their simple joy in living, the youthful comments, help fill gaping holes in our hearts. We want to hug them forever.*

How rejuvenating it is to have a simple visit with young and healthy people. Caregivers, caught in the nightmare of the deathwatch, sometimes forget that life, indeed, does go on.

*It is a wonderful day. We are reluctant to return, but duty calls. The goodbye hugs are fierce. "Let us know when..." They cannot finish. It is too difficult to say aloud, "when Grandma dies."*

After a refreshing break, the return to duties may be silent. No need to speak. We all know what awaits in the near future.

*Mother is catching angels. I watch as she reaches out again and again. Her fingers close on nothing visible to me. Yet her face is serene, peaceful.*

As the time draws near, scripture verses become more meaningful. God has given his angels a command about our loved ones. They fly watch over them, guarding until heaven is ready.

*Betty is sick. Len believes Dave's "unreasonable rules" are responsible for my sister's illness. So, no visitors tonight. Thank you, God, for small favors.*

Caregivers find that company is a comfort most of the time. The chatter, the warm hugs, the donated food, are all wonderfully supporting. Yet, too much of a good thing is a mixed blessing. We all need some silent time, free from endless questions and the pressing need to be polite. An empty living room may seem like a blessed shrine. We can read the Bible, pray, or even snooze.

> *The telephone awakens both of us. Dave chats with our children while I assemble Mother's evening meds. As I bend over her averted face and gently brush back the soft hair from her forehead, I notice something on the pillow— Mother's upper plate. Tears blur my vision.*
>
> *Why do the little losses affect us so much? It is silly to weep because her false teeth won't stay in. The pride thing again. I attempt to shove the plastic teeth back into her mouth. She falls into an uneasy sleep, her mouth agape, eyes fluttering. The false teeth slide again to the pillow. My hands shake as I add the upper plate to its mate in the pink case. I step away and stare down at the suffering woman. The transformation is complete.*

When the dying person no longer even faintly resembles our loved one, is it easier to accept? We stare at the stranger in our loved one's bed. The face is not familiar. The gray skin is shriveled and darkened, the eyes sunken far into the bony skull. The nose is no longer fleshy but hooks sharply toward the puckered mouth. The body, once plump and rounded, is now a wasted skeleton, skin over sharp bones, barely alive. The skin may have strange spots, translucent circles like tiny skinned-over caves. They look like channels into the inner body. We think we can peek into these openings and view the very structure of the bones. This is not our loved one. This is a dying stranger. Is it easier to feel compassion for this stranger? Yes, if it frees us from tangled parent-child rebellions.

*No longer tied to old habits of resentment and reluctant fidelity, affection overwhelms me. I smooth her soft hair away from her face again and again. I cannot touch her enough. Tears blind my eyes. I am shaken with sobs of regret. Why did it take me so long to express love for my mother? Now, when she is beyond reasonable communication, I yearn for the sound of her voice. We have been angry with each other too long. Is it too late to say, "I love you, Mumma"? She rolls one wild eye in my direction and seems to nod. Maybe it is just a sleeping spasm of head or neck, but I am comforted. Dave finds me weeping. He leads me away.*

❦

*Please, Lord, enough. End his/her suffering. Angels of God, guard and protect our loved one. Bear him/her up into the kingdom. Heavenly Host, welcome him/her with open arms.*

# Chapter 36

*"Give her eternal rest, O Lord,*
*and may your light shine on her for ever."*
*Song of Farewell,*
Order of Christian Funerals

Funeral rites in the Catholic Church no longer burden the spirit of mourners with black vestments and droning Latin dirges. Today's funerals, modified by changes from Vatican II, are a celebration of the rebirth of the soul into heavenly light. The music is so beautiful, that we may find ourselves singing snatches of it as we go about daily chores.

> *My soft humming soothes Mother as I work to make her more comfortable. When her groans change to a "Pah!" of bitter disgust, I know she needs a diaper change. She squirms away from the soiled diaper. She thinks anything to do with normal bodily functions is dirty. I hum as I work to alleviate her embarrassment.*

Diarrhea in a comatose patient presents an additional problem. Caregivers may wonder if morphine suppositories remain in the intestinal tract long enough to kill pain.

> *Before I leave for church, I give her an ounce of liquid morphine. The suppositories are running low. Time to call Hospice again. I have to stroke her throat before she swal-*

*lows. The gulp of the medicine hitting bottom reminds me of how empty her stomach must be. I vow to try to make her eat something later. Maybe a milkshake?*

Caregivers often walk a fine line between good nursing care, and trying to play God. When patients refuse food, is it right to force-feed them? Will nourishing foods make our loved ones more comfortable, or unnecessarily prolong their agony? Our loved one may be rigid, locked into the endless battle, sucking in breath and holding it. *O God! How long?*

*When I return from church, Mother is restless. Her nightgown and the sheets are soaked with dank sweat. She rolls from side to side, a limp stranger, as I change the bedding. She has a strong odor. I lift her arms and smooth baby powder into her armpits. As I hold one of her hands aloft, she gives my fingers a faint squeeze. I smile, touched by her brief gesture of affection. "You smell as if you put in a hard day's work, Mother." My feeble joke turns her face toward me. Her gaping mouth and sightless gaze sting my eyes. So old! So much pain. She blinks, then scowls. "Go away! I'm hot!"*

When loved ones speak after days of silence, we are stunned. Their first clear words in days! It matters not that they are the familiar crabby patient. Maybe this is a remission?

*In our case, when I return with a milkshake, Mother is comatose again. Her eyes stare at the ceiling as angels fly past. Her head turns to watch them as they circle. I finger the sopping nightie. Funny how sweaty she is on such a cool day. Even with the furnace running, it is drafty in the house. Her unusual attack of the sweats does not alarm me.*

Caregivers may not realize that a soaking sweat signals

the acute shock that precedes death. If we knew how close the patients are to sweet relief, we would sit beside them watching and waiting for Jesus to come.

> *Instead, I assuage my attack of the shakes by grabbing a quick sandwich. After lunch, I check Mother again. She seems peaceful watching her invisible angels. I hit the couch for a quick nap before noon meds. As soon as my head touches the pillow, the phone rings. A relative offers comfort and sympathy. "Let us know..." she says. I hang up and snuggle into the yellow blanket.*

Sometimes the first hint of your loved one's victory is the silence of the house. It is quiet. Too quiet. The furnace is silent. No clocks tick aloud. You can't even hear your loved one's labored breathing.

> *I raise my head, waiting for the inevitable snort and snore of her resumed struggle to breathe. Nothing. The yellow blanket tangles around my feet as I leap off the couch. I stand in the hallway and stare into the sickroom. Mother no longer watches her angels. Her dark gaze is fixed on the far wall where Jesus hangs on a large crucifix. Her mouth gapes open in eternal surprise. She does not draw another breath.*

What do our loved ones see, we wonder, as we weep over the still body. Flocks of angels, their wings bearing them up? Jesus coming to welcome them home? Your body twitches with panicked thoughts of so many things to do. Call the relatives. Notify Hospice. Call the mortuary. Put teeth back in. Do not give in to the frantic busywork of denial. None of these things is important right now. There will be lots of time later for the official duties of death.

> *Later is soon enough to pick out a becoming dress for her final party. Tomorrow will bring a gathering of mourners and*

*flowers. The day after that will see her placed beside Dad in their shared resting place. But today, right now, it is more important to sit and contemplate my peaceful mother. Now it is enough to hold her still warm hand, and to allow the grace of her blessed release wash over me. To watch the pain lines in her face relax, smoothed by joyous acceptance, until she is once more the serene mother of my childhood.* Father Bob was right. It is beautiful!

Death releases caregivers too. No longer will we have to agonize with each labored breath. No longer will we doubt our decision to refuse our loved ones the euthanasia they begged for.

*I remember how she begged us to kill her, just one week ago. My heart swells with grateful relief that we waited for God to take her. Now it is time to pray and give thanks. To rejoice in her final victory over pain. And to sing Mumma home.*

Saints of God, come to her aid!
Hasten to meet her, angels of the Lord!
Receive her soul and present her to God the Most High.
(Song of Farewell, *Order of Christian Funerals*)

*Dave, just back from church, walks in. I give her a final kiss. "Good-bye Mumma. Go with God."*